Life Behind

The Mask

Umpire's Stories from Youth Baseball

by Michael Schafer

The names have been changed to protect the innocent or, in some cases, the guilty.

MS154 Publications
1010 10th Avenue West
Bradenton, FL 34205

ISBN-13: 978-1541389472

ISBN-10: 1541389476

Cover Illustrated by Al Musitano

Manufactured in the United States

Dedication:

This book is dedicated to all the fathers who have taken the time to work and play with their children and teach them the game of baseball. Especially, though, it is dedicated to my father, Robert 'Buck' Schafer, who not only taught my brother and me how to play the game of baseball but also how to officiate it. Every time I step onto the field to adjudicate a game, I think of him and the hundreds of other men and women who have umpired youth baseball games. Hopefully some of these players will someday follow suit and help the next generation of baseball players. We are only 'paying forward', folks.

Life Behind The Mask

Introduction

After more than forty years of umpiring youth baseball, many people encouraged me, "there has to be a book in there somewhere." It's been fun for me and I wanted to add to the players' enjoyment of the game.

I umpired youth baseball for several reasons. When my older brother, Robert, and I were too old to play youth baseball ourselves, our father, our teams' manager for several years, stepped into umpiring in order to stay in the game. Bob and I just naturally followed him and put on the tools of ignorance, as the catcher's and umpire's equipment is called – a natural step for me as I loved playing the catcher position. As an umpire, though, I needed to remember not to pick up the loose ball when the catcher dropped it. Been there, done that. My bad. Until a few years ago, when the catcher wasn't ready to take warm-up pitches between innings, if the managers didn't mind, I'd throw on the glove and take a few pitches, even occasionally throwing down to second base, just to prove to myself after all these years, I could still hit that put-out spot as I was taught: about the size of a quarter, three feet to the first-base-side of second. Some people may think it unprofessional. My intent was showing the managers, the parents, and the kids there's no job on that field I felt above doing. However, once I moved to Florida, for the most part I stopped the practice. A manager objected, saying I was coaching one team's pitcher by giving him the catcher's mitt as a target to hit for a strike. It only takes one complaint to make waves. So I stopped. At least for a while.

The second reason for being an umpire is because I love it. Through the years coaches and parents have said I seem to have as much fun as the players. Is it that obvious? I learned from the best instructor possible – my father. Following his time in the U.S. Navy during World War II, Dad played semi-pro ball in Ohio. That is until an errant line drive came up and smacked him upside the head during pre-game warm-ups. The impact impaired the peripheral vision in his right eye and his playing days were done. But he still wanted to pass along some knowledge to his two sons and their friends. So he became our team manager.

His name was Robert but, because there were so many Roberts and Bobs around the ball fields, he went by Buck. Everyone knew Buck and knew his first interest focused on the players and their having a positive attitude toward the sport and life. At the end of every practice, every game, he would gather all the players together. With their parents standing nearby, he would collectively ask us three questions: (1) Did you have fun? (2) Did you learn anything? (3) Are you coming back tomorrow? If we could answer yes to those three questions, we had a good day. It didn't matter if we won or not, it didn't matter who made what mistake during that game or practice. He taught us to look for the positive in every opportunity. You learn from every error, every out you've made just as much as from every hit and base reached safely. I've tried to pass that message along to the youth I've encountered over the years. And to their parents.

I prefer to officiate the games at the younger levels. These youngsters still play a game. When you get up to the thirteen-to fifteen-year-old divisions, they're interested in how they personally did during the game. At the high school levels, it's become a very serious sport for them. Batting averages and earned runs count with vital importance. That eighth of an inch of the ball that just cut across the bottom corner of the strike zone had better be called the strike the pitcher threw it to be. And there is no such thing as a runner and the ball getting to the base at the same time when that runner knows he got there first and isn't afraid to stand in the umpire's face to convince him. Or at least try to intimidate him. (By the way, there is no such thing as a tie between the runner and the baseball. The runner must beat the ball to the bag. If it's a tie, he didn't beat it.)

So I stay in the younger levels where the players (both boys and girls) are still learning to play the game and sometimes forget what to do when they've hit the ball. I've seen the nine-year-old second baseman in the set position as the pitch comes in to the batter and never move a muscle as the batted ball scoots across the ground no more than ten feet to his left and on into right field.

Unfortunately, the parents of the younger players cause most of the problems. Tommy may be accepting of the idea he just let strike three cross the heart of the plate without ever taking the bat off his shoulder but his mom in the bleachers is certainly going to let "Blue" know she could see from there the pitch was actually ball four. Half in jest I've said the greatest game is one where there are no spectators or know-it-all coaches but just the kids playing the game. As a youngster, I played many a sandlot game like that and any name calling was all in fun.

There was a game just a few years ago where the spectators shouted across the backstop at each other. The comments were discourteous to say the least and, in some cases, downright disgusting to myself and these young players. The players on the field behaved better than the spectators in the stands.

Finally, I'd heard all of the abuse directed at me, the coaches for both teams and the players themselves, that I would tolerate. With a batter in the box and an active count on him, I stepped out in front of the catcher, took off my mask and stood on home plate to address the spectators behind the backstop. "Parents," I began my brief sermon, "we are here to watch and encourage these young people as they mature in playing together nicely. Unfortunately your behavior here is something worse than I feel they need to see.

"Now, if you cannot behave in a respectable manner, I

invite you to leave. And if the behavior and comments continue, it will no longer be an invitation." I indicated the players on the field and in the dugouts. "These youngsters have learned how to play together nicely. Let's not show them how to behave like spoiled brats, please."

I returned to my position behind the catcher, shaking like a leaf while trying to put my mask back on. I feared the obscene comments would continue or even intensify. Fortunately, all I heard from behind me as I set myself for the pitcher to continue was soft talking with comments like, "You know, he's right." This was a night where just knowing the baseball rulebook wasn't enough. I also had to use a little crowd control.

Not everyone who knows the game of baseball can be an umpire and, regrettably, not everyone who is an umpire knows the rules of the game. I have seen chapters where, once a young man reaches sixteen, he wants to become an umpire and feels he knows the rules because he's played for a few years. One young man told me, with all seriousness, he never wasted his time reading the rulebook. "Everything's so clear cut here," he told me. As you are about to see, nothing could be further from the truth.

No matter who you are, if you want to be an umpire, your first assignment is to get a current rulebook and read it from cover to cover, section by section, rule by rule. Then read it again – and again – and again – until you understand the applications of the rules, know and understand all of the "exceptions" and "unless" instances and can apply and enforce them on the spot in the heat of a game.

Generally, the umpire is the only paid individual on the field, although several chapters rely entirely on volunteer umpires and I am active in those as well. The youngsters play for the experience and teamwork of the sport. The managers and coaches, usually the parents of some of the kids, want their sons (or daughters) to get their lion's share of playing time, whether their ability deserves it or not. The umpire becomes the only unbiased voice of adjudication present. Payment for a couple hours work could be from ten to fifty dollars per game depending on the league and level of play.

If you thought umpires were rich, that's just not so. If I wanted the big bucks, I could have moved up to a professional minor league. The fact that I'm still here shows I'm dedicated more to the kids.

In some chapters, umpires receive no payment at all. Those rely solely on volunteers coming to the fields or randomly picking a fan from the stands to officiate the game. Unfortunately, in many cases, the umpiring is often not consistent and sometimes blatantly unfair for one side or the other. Consequently, it teaches the youngsters little about sportsmanship or the game. I've stepped into such chapters to offer a truly unbiased set of eyes. And, yes, to have a little fun myself.

During summer months, my umpiring gear stayed in my car. It occurred while at work, I would get a call from the Umpire-In-Chief needing an umpire on my night off. Could I take another game? Somebody bailed out of an assignment or gotten sick or injured at work or had to work over and couldn't make a game and a replacement was needed. So I would go straight from work to the field, change from my office clothes and into the umpiring equipment in the field's restroom (sometimes nothing more than a portable toilet) and get behind the plate for a game.

A few years ago, living in Akron, I had a night off from umpiring. I decided to go to a field where I'd never officiated, near the Akron Municipal Airport and Derby Downs, just to watch a game from the bleachers. Arriving at the field about a quarter till six, I noticed there was no umpire present for the six o'clock contest.

I never said a word but one of the team managers recognized me even in street clothes. He asked if I were there to do his game. "No," I explained, "I'm here to watch one for a change." However, when six o'clock became five after the hour and still no umpire, the question became, "Would you umpire this game?" I don't say no too often regarding baseball so I went to my car and put on my gear. I would still watch a game but it would be from the familiar perspective of behind the mask. Mine is a life behind the mask.

Admittedly, this collection of baseball experiences is not all humorous because there are times the Grand Old Game does have bad memories. Players occasionally get hurt. People lose their tempers. Harsh words are sometimes exchanged. One benefit of being a kid is usually within twenty-four hours, if even that long, all is forgotten (except maybe broken bones and those take a little longer). Only when we get older we might hold on to something a little longer. If a manager or coach or even a player angered me during a game or I had to eject a participant for improper conduct or language, in all seriousness, by the next game it's all forgotten on my side and everyone starts with a clean slate. Now, if that person wants to make a point of it later in the season, my first reaction is to have totally forgotten the confrontation (which is mostly the truth). If he or she persists however, believe me, I can reach into my mental file cabinet and recall the minutest detail of the facts leading up to the ejection and remind that individual of things he or she may have chosen not to remember. Thankfully, it's only happened twice and, after the first reminder, the offense was forgotten by both parties for the rest of the season.

This is a game for the kids and we must remember everyone at the field is there for the kids' benefit. I don't want to see them behave like spoiled children when they don't get their way. They've already matured past that point in their lives and I see no reason to go back to it on the ball field. Besides, for two hours each evening, I get to forget about my adult job and be a kid again myself.

Life Behind The Mask

So, sit back, get comfortable and enjoy this recitation of events I've witnessed during my years as an umpire for Ohio Hot Stove, community recreational, Little League, Babe Ruth and Cal Ripken League, and AAU Baseball as well as some tales from my playing days in the early '60s and much, much more.

Some will make you chuckle, some will make you wonder what the people involved were thinking, some may double you up with laughter as they did me at the time, and some just might bring a tear to your eye (and we won't tell anyone if it was a happy tear or not).

Let's Get Started

This is baseball at its most fundamental. The rules specify the dimensions of the field, the size and weight of the baseball and bats, the limitations of the gloves for the pitcher, the first baseman, the catcher and the remainder of the players. It states the game is to be played between two teams at a time and explains the defensive team has nine participants active on the field while the offense may have no more than four at a time. Each team is under the direction of a managerial staff to provide direction, coaching and support. And, above everyone else on the field, the rulebook places the responsibility on the umpires (at least one and up to six) to adjudicate those rules and keep the game moving along in an orderly fashion.

The object of the game is to get more runs than your opponent and win the contest. Imagine that. How to score a run is probably the simplest part of the rules of the game to understand. Then why is the second most asked question during the course of a game "Does that run count?" when a player touches home plate during a play that resulted in the third out? And it can be asked multiple times during the same game. The logical answer is because most managers (or players for that matter) have not taken the time to read the rulebook before stepping onto the field for that first practice session or any time during the season.

Our dad, Buck, taught my brother and me to know the rules of the game before we attempted to interpret them in action. It would not be uncommon for dinner conversation at home to revolve around a knotty problem one of us come across on the playing field or even dreamed up ourselves.

Momma permitted the discussions because she could see that Buck, Bob, and I enjoyed the sport. Our older sister, Lucindia (but everyone called her Lu for short), would also enter into conversations. She served as scorekeeper for the teams when Bob and I played and later played on a women's slow-pitch softball team. For a few years Buck served as manager of that team, but that's another story.

As far as a run counting, the easiest way to answer the question is when an offensive player safely reaches first, second, third, and home base in order before the defensive team records three outs on the offensive team, that is a run.

Now, unfortunately there is an exception to that explanation. If the runner accomplishes the base running but reaches home plate during the same play when the third out is recorded, there are certain stipulations to be met to count that run. If the runner crosses home plate, whether forced to or not, in the same play when the batter/runner is put out before reaching first base, that runs does not count. Or if any other runner is forced out at a base, or if a preceding runner misses a base in the same play and is put out for the third out of the half-inning, then that run does not count. Are you confused yet? I thought so.

Simply put, if the runner legally touches home base in the same play where the third out is made by force-out, the run does not count. It doesn't matter if he touched the base before the out was made as long as it was in one continuous play. However, if the batter/runner is retired on a base other than first or is put out after touching first base safely, score that run. Still confused?

Case in point: With the bases loaded and two out, the batter blasts a hit deep over the right fielder's head. As the only umpire for this twelve-year-old and under contest, I positioned myself off the baseline between home and third to view all the runners as they touched each base and watched the ball come in from right field. The runners from third and second scored easily as the batter/runner hustled around the bases. When the throw came into the second baseman who had stepped out towards right field to accept the cut-off throw, the batter/runner was touching second and took two steps towards third while clapping his hands (whether applauding himself or trying to distract the fielder was irrelevant).

The runner originally from first was now on his way to home plate. The catcher screamed for the ball to be thrown to him for the play at the plate and the second baseman complied. But the throw was late and the sliding runner safe. However, the batter/runner headed for third as the alert catcher fired the ball down to the fielder covering. The runner attempted to stop only to slip on the loose dirt and was tagged out for the third out of the inning.

I walked over to each bench to be sure the scorekeepers knew to count all three runs as valid. A good thing because the manager of the defensive team was telling his scorekeeper none of the runs counted during the same play resulting in the third out.

"Not quite," I explained. "You actually had at least three different plays there. The hit for the double was one, the attempt at home was two and the putout at third was three. Since all three runners crossed the plate before the third out was made, all three runs scored." To say the least, he was not happy, but he had to agree with my logic. So does the rulebook.

*　　*　　*

The Ohio Hot Stove Baseball League is divided into several divisions of play based upon the ages of the players in two-year brackets. When I was a player back in the 1960s, the divisions started at the age of nine for players in what was called "H" League. These players were just learning the game and sometimes didn't understand all of the rules. Many of the managers understood them even less and didn't instill the positive attitude Buck taught us.

For the lower age levels there's usually only one umpire, positioned behind the catcher with full equipment. Believe me there would be no way I'd step onto the field without proper equipment and certainly not behind the catcher. In the early years of my umpiring career, we used the outside chest protector commonly used by the Major League American League umpires at the time and had to carry it all around the field with us as we made calls. The benefit of this type of protector was it could be moved between the umpire and the ball when it got past the catcher. The down side is it was bulky and often times in the way as we hustled out to a base to adjudicate a close play with a throw coming in from the outfield.

Originally, these chest protectors were nothing more than a piece of foam about two inches thick covered with the black material. Later, an air-filled bladder replaced the foam, and provided a little more security.

Around the mid-1980s, I personally switched to the inside protector similar in design to the catcher's gear and worn underneath the umpire's shirt. It affords the umpire more mobility while still providing most of the protection as the larger item.

For this lowest age-level of play, we have what is called a Mercy Rule. If a team is ahead by ten or more runs after five complete innings, the game is ruled as completed (standard games for the two youngest age brackets in Hot Stove are seven innings; the Mercy Rule is applied at the end of four innings for the six-inning Little League contests). In more than a few games, I applied the Mercy Rule.

Another rule is all players present must play at least six defensive outs and get one at-bat. In other words, usually in the top of the third inning, the substitute players were inserted into the lineup and were well-rested compared to the players in throughout the contest. There may be only one or two substitute players, but there could be as many as six as the absolute maximum roster size was fifteen players. (The size of the rosters would fluctuate from season to season and from league to league being anywhere from ten to fifteen.) The down side of this rule is these players were sometimes not as skilled as the starters. They may have been the younger players or those not as coordinated or able to throw the ball as far or as accurately as the starters.

But they got to play in order to attempt to build up their abilities and their confidence. Some managers were inventive enough to start the subs and insert the better players in the third inning, but not too many really got that serious about winning at this lower level, thankfully.

In one specific game the visiting team just overpowered the home team and had outscored them in every inning. The home team scored only one run in four innings while their opponent had collected twenty-two tallies. Even with their substitute players inserted, they still added to their lead.

As we entered the bottom of the fifth inning, I visited the home team's bench area to let the manager know the score. "Your boys need to score at least twelve runs in this half-inning or that's game."

One of the youthful players overheard me. "We've only scored one run all game. How can we score twelve runs in a half-inning?" he said despairingly.

The manager told his players, they could score the runs by hitting the ball and listening to the coaches. He was being positive for the players.

I smiled to myself as I returned to home plate and called, "Batter up!"

I noticed the new pitcher for the visiting team was not as sharp as the previous two players used by this team. I gave the batter an extra moment to get ready as I brushed off home plate. With my back to the pitcher, I stood up and looked at the batter and just said, "Watch the ball hit the bat and run to first base. Okay?" He nodded his head and got set in the batter's box.

The first two pitches were well outside the strike zone. The next one actually hit the ground before crossing the plate just above the batter's shoe tops. I called time and stepped out in front of home plate to clean it off again. I told the batter the count was 3-and-0 and quietly told him "unless this pitch is right down the middle, don't swing."

Life Behind The Mask

Yes, I was being a coach but I didn't care. I really don't think the catcher could hear the conversation. Besides I wasn't telling this batter any secrets of the game.

I returned to my position behind the catcher, set the mask on my face and ducked down behind my big outside chest protector. "Play ball!"

The pitcher came to a set position with no runners on and delivered the pitch. It was slow and it was straight and it was right over the plate. The batter swung and lifted the ball to left field. He ran to first and didn't stop until he slid safely into second base.

The next batter walked but the third pitch got away from the catcher and the runner advanced to third. This pitcher was not able to throw fast and accurately at the same time. If he got it over the plate, it was slow enough for the batter to crush it. If he threw fast, more often than not, it was outside the strike zone and many times too wide even for the catcher to stop. Fortunately, at this field the backstop wasn't more than a dozen feet behind the plate.

When the lead-off batter came up to the plate a second time in the same inning, I cleaned off home plate again and asked him, "How many?" He knew exactly what I meant and answered, "Seven."

I looked at my indicator to see there were still no outs in the inning.

When he came around a third time, I didn't need to ask. He told me, "Fifteen," but this time there was one out and I wasn't sure if he'd made it. To this player, though, it wouldn't have mattered because now he was having fun.

The other team? Not so much. Their manager could not substitute his starting players back in to stop the bleeding. He'd already changed the pitcher for the left fielder, but he wasn't much better. At least he was getting the ball over the plate more. But the offensive team was also hitting it more frequently, and to places the defensive players weren't positioned. The fielders frequently threw the ball to a wrong base or held on to it too long to make a successful play.

When this same batter stepped in for a fourth at-bat in the same inning, it had gotten rather dark as the game had started around 5:30, and there were no lights on this field. I turned to the bench and asked, "How many runs have you guys scored this inning?"

The scorekeeper took a few seconds to count them all up. "Twenty-two." That put them in the lead.

I turned to the center fielder and held up a ball for him to see. "Center fielder, catch this ball," I called and threw it out toward him. He moved to his right but my throw was to his left.

It fell untouched to the ground. "Could you see the ball?" I shouted.

"Where is it?" he asked.

"This game is called on account of darkness," I declared. "The home team has taken the lead in the bottom of the inning. This game is over." These boys had come back from a whopping deficit to win the game by a run. They not only scored the twelve runs needed to keep playing, they scored enough to win the game. To this day, I still get choked up thinking of that game. (Got a box of tissues handy?)

* * *

I won't go into the specifics of the playing field rule here because, frankly, it takes nearly five pages in the Official Baseball Rulebook. Also, for the different age divisions of play, there are different sized fields.

The youngest players, under ten years old, have base paths of only sixty feet, not the Major League ninety feet. Move up one age bracket to the eleven-and twelve-year-olds and that extends to seventy feet. Those fields having outfield fences, may be no less than 200 feet from home plate for the under ten bracket and 210 for the next grouping. Similarly, the distance from home plate to the pitching rubber changes.

Because of the limits to the number of baseball fields built and maintained in most municipalities, usually these two lower age brackets are forced to share the same fields. On Monday and Wednesday, the youngest division might play; on Tuesday and Thursday, the next division schedules games. Fridays were saved for make-ups of rained out games or completion of suspended games.

In Ohio Hot Stove Baseball the lowest division was called "H" League (although I've been told they have since added an "H1" League for players aged seven and eight, and an "I" League for instructional games for players under seven) and the eleven-and twelve-year-old's division was called "G" League. In Little League the brackets are divided into Minor League for seven-to twelve-year-old and Major League for nine-to twelve-year-old. (What you see on TV for their World Series is the Major League division.)

Using the same field can be a challenge but good old-fashioned American ingenuity solves the problem . . . to a degree. On fields with no outfield fences and no elevated pitcher's mound, the solution involved using a permanent location for home plate and just move the bases out farther while installing two pitching rubbers *sans* elevated mounds in the center of the infield. This may solve the problem for the maintenance of the field but does present a few interesting dilemmas for the players. On more than one occasion I have had a ten-year-old pitcher throwing from the upper league pitching rubber. The situation is usually not noticed until the manager makes the first trip out to the mound to talk with his pitcher. Technically it makes every pitch thrown up to that point an illegal pitch because he wasn't in contact with the appropriate rubber when he released the ball to the plate. I have never attempted to create that penalty (because once the next pitch is thrown, the previous play is official in the scorebooks). We just put the pitcher on the correct rubber and proceed from there. I'll give him a few warm-up throws to get himself acclimated to the correct distance and it's usually good to go from there. In fact, if he was throwing strikes from the further rubber, he would have no problem adjusting to the correct distance.

It is when the "G" League player is using his proper rubber that we find the most problems. In coming forward to deliver the ball, his step toward the batter can sometimes be directly on top of the younger league's pitching rubber. This can be a potentially dangerous situation for players with rubber spikes. The two easiest solutions I have used over the years are (1) Attempt to keep a constant supply of dirt to cover the closer rubber and allow the pitcher to step onto that dirt and not the exposed pitcher's plate, and (2) When necessary and where possible, remove the closer pitcher's rubber and fill in that location with dirt and sand for the game. Whenever choice two was used, it was done under my supervision and we made sure the plate was returned to the proper location for the next night's game before we left. Now, because of vandalism and the pitching rubbers being removed from the diamonds, most fields now have the pitching rubber attached to a cement slab under the dirt and it cannot be removed. Those fields mandate using the first solution. The other problem is the older league player using the younger league's pitching rubber. This is much easier to discern and correct. Obviously, if that pitch is coming in quicker than the players and this umpire are accustomed to, I will take a walk out to the pitcher to check the plate. Now I usually do a walk around on the field before game time anyway and try to be mindful of the starting pitchers when they start their warm-ups so I have an idea of whether they are using the correct rubber or not, but doubtless there have been times when someone has a question just before the game starts requiring my attention. If there is a two-man umpire crew, the task of

Life Behind The Mask

checking on the pitcher falls to the field umpire and the home plate umpire can deal with the questions. But with the usual one-man crew, that umpire must become a jack-of-all-trades and sometimes something may slip through the cracks in pre-game preparations.

On fields with permanent outfield fences, the solution for the base problem must be a little more inventive. There is the easy way—set the fences to the 210-foot distance from home plate and reset the bases and pitching rubbers just like the previous fields. Or there is the engineering way—install two home plates, two base paths such that the home plate closer to the pitcher's rubber is for the lower league and the one farther back is for the upper division. This, of course, means that the catcher for the younger division now becomes the one standing on the home plate for the upper division and there are two sets of foul lines and two base paths for the umpire to judge on the same field (although obviously not at the same time) and the home run fence for the younger division is a little farther than minimum regulation but they can still clear it with a little extra effort.

Which way is better for each instance is not for me to say. I am not a landscaper or an outdoor designer. I just have to have a real good idea of what's going on where as the game progresses. Sometimes during a game I am reminded of Abbot and Costello's "Who's on First?" and think that might actually be easier than what I am doing. But I am doing this for the kids. And I love it.

* * *

I've mentioned before how one community answered the question of two different age divisions using the same fields, though on different nights, by installing two home plates and widening the field for the older division. During that previous segment, I said the only player really disadvantaged by this situation was the catcher in the younger division because he would have to set up on top of

17

the home plate for the older division. Well, a few nights ago I was proven wrong. Yes, this umpire is admitting he was wrong. At least in this case.

A ten-year-old and younger division game with runners on first and third and only one out, the ball got away from the catcher, to the backstop. Like any good base runners, both players took off to advance. And, like any good pitcher, the young player on the mound came up to cover home plate and get set for the throw from the catcher who, like any good catcher, hastened to retrieve the baseball from the backstop. Everything was set for a close play at home plate and this umpire, like any good umpire, was set to make the call.

Except something just didn't look right.

The ball came in from the catcher but was not down on the plate for an easy tag. Instead he tossed it toward the pitcher's chest. He needed to raise his glove to catch the ball just as the runner slid in to home plate. But I didn't call him safe. Remember I said something just wasn't right? This ten-year-old pitcher set up to cover the older division's home plate and the runner slid into the plate the pitcher was protecting.

The ball came in high, so the pitcher was late with the tag as the runner slid over the base under the tag. And I had to call him out. The offensive team manager, coaching at third base, charged down the line.

"What do you mean he's out?" he challenged me. "He was sitting on home plate before that tag was ever applied."

The runner, still in a seated position, looked up at me. Surveying the scene, I couldn't argue with what the manager said. All I could do was to step around the player on the ground and, with a swipe of my foot, clear off the home plate the runner should be sitting upon. I pointed to the correct plate and cleared my throat to indicate this was where he needed to slide in order to be safe.

"But the pitcher was back here. My boy just went to that

base. You can't blame him for their pitcher going to the wrong base."

"Not my fault, coach," I said. "I can't tell him, 'Hey, son, you're on the wrong base.'"

As the runner stood up off the base and walked to his dugout, the manager pondered my words for a minute, trying to formulate an argument in his favor. "Well," he finally decided, "can't you give it to him? I mean, he *did* beat the throw. He'd been safe if he slid into the right base." By this time the other team's manager joined the conference just in time to hear his counterpart plead, "Close enough is good enough, right?"

Doing my best to suppress a chuckle, I turned to the defense's manager. "Well, coach, what do you think? Is close enough good enough?"

I could see he found humor in the idea. "Yeah, sure," he agreed. "As long as it goes both ways." He pointed to first base. "So if my batter is close enough to first base when the ball gets there, that's good enough, right?"

"No, no, no." Manager 'A' waved his arms. "That's not what I meant at all." He turned again to me. "It's just so confusing to have two bases out here like this." He stepped forward and, with his foot, pushed some dirt over the back plate. For a moment I was afraid I was going to have a Billy-Martin moment with dirt being kicked on my shoes. Dejectedly the manager accepted the futility of his actions and, with chin resting on his sternum, walked back to the third base coach's box with two outs now recorded against his team. At least he had a runner on third base since no one paid any attention to the runner who had started from first.

And, for the record, managers, there is no rule saying 'close enough is good enough' and I don't foresee the rulebook being changed any time soon to include it.

*　　*　　*

Life Behind The Mask

There are few aspects of the game of baseball not covered by the official Major League rulebook. Even the dimensions of the playing field are specified, at least to the minimums of the outfield fences. An exception is included for older stadiums built before 1958.

Newer parks must have outfield fences a minimum of 325 feet on the foul line and straight away center field needs to be no less than 400 feet from home plate. Otherwise, special permission needs to be obtained from the Office of the Commissioner.

No youth player could hit those distances, but I have seen quite a few easily reach the 210-foot distances common at the fields with fence enclosures. A few seasons ago in spring ball in Florida, in a ten-to twelve-year-old's contest, the third batter of the inning came to the plate with two out and no one on. This player would swing at practically anything thrown. Yes, when he made contact, the ball traveled and he would get on base. He probably also led his team in strikeouts for swinging at pitches out of the strike zone. I expected this to be a one-two-three inning.

The first pitch was over the batter's head but he still swung at it. As the catcher retrieved the ball from the backstop, I silently indicated strike one. The next pitch came outside and wide of the plate. The batter took a lazy swing with only one hand on the bat and fouled it off toward the first base dugout. Strike two.

When this was the time to waste a pitch just off the outside corner of the plate, the pitcher decided to send one right down the center. And the batter decided to send the ball over the right field fence for a home run. With the ball over the fence, I watched the young man trot around the bases before tossing another game ball from my pouch to the pitcher.

The next batter stepped in as I heard someone from the bench offer, "I bet you can't hit it over the fence."

Continuing to look straight ahead at the pitcher, I shook

Life Behind The Mask

my finger at the bench in general and good-naturedly reminded them, "No betting in baseball, boys." It brought a chuckle as the game proceeded. No more than four pitches into this next player's turn, he lifted the ball over the right field fence just to the left of where the previous ball disappeared for back-to-back home runs.

As he jogged around the bases, I indicated to the home team bench I needed another baseball. Two were tossed out to me but only one was usable for game conditions. I accepted it and tossed back the other one, indicating it had loose threads on the stitching. The coach acknowledged and dropped it in the bucket where they kept practice balls.

The defensive team manager went out to talk with his pitcher as I brushed off home plate, giving him additional time to calm his young pitcher. Back-to-back home runs were unusual but I had seen them before in my years of umpiring. These would be followed by four pitches wide of the plate to the next batter, the pitcher afraid of throwing another home run offering. Then the pitcher was removed and the game went on. This unseasonably warm spring evening in Florida, the pitcher showed determination to get that third out before any more damage was done.

With two outs already recorded but also two runs, the fifth batter of the inning stepped in. The pitcher attempted to throw a fastball down the center of the plate and the batter obliged him by promptly lifting it over the left center field fence for the third home run in a row.

As his teammates met him at home plate, one of the players brought out another ball for me. He said it was one of those hit over the right field fence. I looked it over and agreed it could be. This time I walked out to the mound. When I put the ball in the pitcher's glove, I said, "I've never seen four home runs in a row and I don't want to start now." I attempted to sound gruff but smiled while I spoke.

"Believe me, I don't want to see that either, Blue." The pitcher chuckled. He was apparently calm and ready to get

21

this next batter. And I had faith he could do it.

When I got back to home plate, the catcher was holding the other game ball from over the fence. I accepted it and placed it in my pouch. Two pitches later, I removed it as the batter fouled off the pitch out of play to the right. Two more pitches and two more foul balls contained within the playing field and the foul ball was tossed back to me.

After this batter fouled off seven pitches, extending a 1-2 count to double-digit pitches, he connected with the ball, placing it to the right of the right field line but still over the fence. I tossed the remaining game ball to the pitcher and indicated to him the 1-2 count then showed him there were two out. A clenched fist to indicate to him to keep coming to the plate and I returned to behind the catcher. I really wanted to see this pitcher get out of this jam. I also didn't want to see a fourth home run in a row against him.

Unfortunately, two pitches later, that was exactly what I saw. The batter connected with a change-up and placed it over the right-center field fence with enough distance to clear a 220-foot fence.

Thankfully, the seventh batter grounded out to the second baseman for the third out, but the damage was done with back-to-back-to-back-to-back home runs. I've never seen it before and don't want to see it again. It's good for the offensive team but completely takes the wind out of the sails of a youthful pitcher and his teammates.

As the team walked off the field, I did something I seldom do. I walked over to meet the pitcher near the third base line. "That's the way I like to see you hang in there," I told him. I offered my fist for a tap and he complied. Then, as we both approached their dugout, to the team in general, I offered, "Now, you guys need to get those runs back." In my mind I wasn't playing favorites; I was just encouraging the players to stay in the game.

The coach picked up on my positive comments and gave encouragement to the players as I spoke with the scorekeeper to see where we were in the game. A blatant excuse of a reason to be there but I wanted to pick those players up before they had an opportunity to let themselves get down.

Always be positive. Right, Buck? And, for the record, I went over to the other team's bench to congratulate the coach for the good offensive inning and extended my hand in good faith.

*   *   *

With the younger players, say ten years old and under, having the right equipment (glove, hat and such) is vital. It goes beyond that, though.

There was, however, this nine-or ten-year-old right-handed pitcher's left shoelace was untied during his warm-up pitches. As the catcher threw the ball down to second base following his last warm-up toss, I pointed out to the youngster the issue and he tied the shoelace. Four or five pitches, and I noticed (from behind home plate, mind you) it loose again, apparently from his leg-kick motion when pitching from a wind-up. Calling time for him to re-tie the lace again was required.

Another batter or two later in the same inning and the lace became loose again. For the fourth or fifth time, I had to call time. I was almost ready to walk out to the mound and double-tie it myself. But a young lady from the stands beat me to it. I could see the young pitcher mouth, "Oh, Mom," as he hung his head in embarrassment. When she finished with the task, she gave him a kiss on his cap for luck. Trying to ease the youngster's embarrassment, I asked, "While we have you out here, does anyone else need their shoelaces tied?"

The spectators chuckled at my attempt at humor and the first baseman took advantage of the opportunity to have his laces knotted. Then the first base coach stuck out his foot as if asking for the mom to tie his shoelace. The spectators loved it and it eased the pitcher's dilemma.

Quite frequently during the course of a game, I will need to call time to allow a player to re-tie his laces. Sometimes a fielder may not even realize the condition, but I make it a point to notice for all players before it becomes an issue. It's always done for their safety. With the arrival of female players, occasionally the time outs also are included for fixing the hair under their caps.

On one occasion, I called time to inform a runner who had just arrived at third base his right shoelace was untied and give him the opportunity to tie it. I noticed the lace being loose as he approached the bag. While the player went about the task, the coach asked, "You could see that from back there?"

"Very little I don't notice."

Shaking his head, he said, "There's nothing wrong with your eyes."

"Keep that in mind for the next strike call."

He chuckled.

At the lower age levels, the kids are out there to have fun but no one ever said I couldn't have a pleasant afternoon, too. It makes the game more enjoyable for everyone. Besides, could you really pick an argument with an umpire who was smiling at you?

Dictionary of Baseball Terms

It's very important to have a shared understanding of the language of the game you are officiating. A few years ago my girlfriend tried to support me by learning some of the basics of the Official Baseball Rulebook. I warned her up front they were sometimes very confusing and a background of a game would be helpful for understand the text. She countered of her experience watching baseball for years and felt she understood. (It sounded strangely like that one youngster who wanted to be an umpire without reading the rulebook.)

After reading less than a page, she asked how anyone could understand these rules when they contradicted themselves. I attempted to explain the three most important words an umpire could learn were "in my judgment." A judgment call cannot be argued. A judgment call cannot be protested. A judgment call is an umpire's interpretation of the rulebook to a specific situation presented on the field. The rules provide a general outlook of the game and the umpire interprets them to the specific situation.

Then I asked her to show me where the book conflicted with itself so early. She pointed to the exception concerning counting the run score during the same play as a third out. She said the rule stated to score a run, the player needed to touch all of the bases in order without being put out. She didn't understand what effect a trailing runner being put out should have on that runner.

I came up with the best means I could think of to explain the situation outside of baseball. My hometown of Alliance, Ohio, was founded in the early nineteenth century at the intersection of at least three passenger and freight railroads in northeastern Ohio and the merger of three villages in the middle of the nineteenth century. Legend has it one of the upper management people, maybe even an owner of one of the railroad companies, coined the term Alliance as the coming together of the railroad tracks in the village.

I explained the runners on the bases are like a railroad train. If one car jumps the tracks, all of the cars are affected. So if one runner is put out, even if he is a trailing runner, it can have an effect on all the rest of the runners. So if the batter/runner is put out before reaching first base, even though the runner coming in from third base already scored before that third out was physically made, his run will not count. If the caboose jumps the track, the engine will not get to where it was going.

*   *   *

The Infield Fly Rule is probably the second most confusing rule in the sport because there are four factors that all must come together for an infield fly to be declared. Two are inarguable, those being the position of the runners at the time of the pitch and the number of outs in the inning. The third point, the ability of an infielder to catch the ball "with ordinary effort" and fourth, what exactly is a fly versus a line drive, are judgment calls. Remember the umpire's three favorite words—"in my judgment."

Simple rule of thumb I and most other umpires use to determine if the hit is a fly or a line drive is: did the ball travel above the fielder's head and then downwards towards him? Fortunately most of the time the hit is a pop-up and easily determined. An exception is a bunt cannot be an infield fly so attention must be paid if an at-bat could have been a bunt.

The "ordinary effort" means no diving catches and no running at breakneck speed to get to a point where a catch *might* be made. Umpiring for so many different age levels caused me problems at times. A fourteen-year-old second baseman could make the catch but the players before me are eleven and under. On more than one occasion I have raised my arm above my head to call an Infield Fly (and by the way, the call should *never* be made until the ball has reached its zenith and is on the way back down to determine if it will be able to be caught by an infielder) and then realized the players of this division couldn't make that catch on their best day. The arm comes down before the voice is raised or I would camouflage the action by adjusting my hat after taking off the mask or some such action. If the ball is dropped, it's very easy to drop the hand into a safe sign with both arms extended out and back numerous times while verbally indicating, "The ball is on the ground! No catch!" Sell that call so there's no doubt you know you're right.

The most humorous instances involve the manager forgetting where his runners were on the bases or the conditions of the Infield Fly Rule.

In the first case in the lower age bracket, when the preceding batter walked, placing runners on first and second and one out, the potential existed for an infield fly. When the second pitch got by the catcher and both runners advanced one base, the potential was gone. (Umpires signal this by stroking the left arm with the right hand to 'wipe off' the rule.) The next pitch was skied "a mile up and a mile straight down" heading for the second baseman. I made no call until the ball was contained in his glove and then called, "Batter's out."

The offensive manager, coaching third base, shouted to me, "Why wasn't that an Infield Fly?"

My answer was quick and factual. I pointed to the right side of the infield and answered, "First base was open, coach."

He'd totally forgotten the runners already advanced. And the managers tell the players to keep their heads in the game?

There are managers who feel, once the umpire calls "infield fly, batter is out," the runners are then free to advance. Not true. If the fielder should drop the ball (or not catch it cleanly as in a normal out situation), the runners do not need to tag up before advancing. The key thing to remember is that regardless whether a fielder catches the ball or not, the batter is still out on an Infield Fly so the runners are not forced to advance.

Of course there is an exception to this rule but it applies only to a batted ball that drops in foul territory. At that point, the ball is foul and the batter is not out. Also, because it is a foul ball, the runners may not advance. If, however, the foul ball is caught, the batter is declared out just as in normal caught foul balls.

Another thing to keep in mind, if the ball that has been declared an Infield Fly lands untouched in fair territory and then bounces or rolls untouched into foul territory before it has passed either first or third base, it is a foul ball.

Now, here comes the worst-case scenario, and fortunately it doesn't happen too many times. If that fly ball falls untouched in foul territory but then bounces into fair territory where it is touched by a fielder, either intentionally or unintentionally, is it, as in normal situations, a fair ball and therefore is considered an Infield Fly? No. It is very important for the fielders to allow a ball to go foul and then touch it as soon as it is completely foul. Or, if it first lands foul, to touch that ball before it has the opportunity of coming back fair. Remember the foul lines are actually part of the playing field and any portion of that ball on or over the line, just like in tennis, is a fair ball.

Several years ago in a high school game with a two-man umpiring crew (as usual I was behind the plate), the contest was between two schools with play-off implications. The bottom of the fifth inning of a close game, with runners on first and second, and only one out. The right-handed batter just took a foul ball off his own left foot for strike two, so I gave him a little extra time to get set in the batter's box. The pitcher, however, was anxious to get this guy out and standing on the pitcher's rubber while I still had my hand extended for "time."

Finally the batter indicated to me that he was ready and, before I dropped my hand, I said to the pitcher, "I don't

Life Behind The Mask

want a quick pitch here. Wait till I call for it." He heard me and gave me one of those "yeah, sure" looks. So I held my hand up until I was set behind the catcher before pointing to the pitcher and calling "Play ball!"

The pitcher was already in the set position without benefit of going through a stretch first and then delivered the pitch. Of course it was a fastball on the outside corner of the plate and about shoulder high. It would have been a ball but the batter took a cut and wound up popping it up towards first base. It was a good height and allowed myself and my umpiring partner to get in the proper positions for the play. Reaching its zenith and traveling back down, I called it: "Infield fly. Batter is out, if fair!" As the first baseman came down the line to catch the ball, stepping across the foul line – left foot out, right foot in, the batter barreled down to first base. By rule, the runner must give the fielder room to make the catch so he moved into foul territory, out of the fielder's way.

As the fielder set up for the catch, he stopped one foot in, one foot out of the field of play. It made no difference if he caught the ball or not, as long as the ball was on the fair side of the line, but the batter suddenly had a loud cough as he passed the fielder, coincidentally right when his opponent was making the catch.

The baseball hit the heel of the glove and bounced off his chest before hitting the ground on the foul side of the line. Without saying a word, I strongly pointed with my left hand to the fair side of the line, indicating the ball had been in fair territory when first touched. Then I raised my right hand in a fist and declared, "Infield fly. Batter is *out!*"

No runners tried to advance but the home team manager came bounding out of his dugout to confront me. "That ball was foul!" he shouted. "You saw it land outside the line! It's foul!"

As calmly as I could, I explained, "It fell off the fielder's glove before hitting the ground."

"But he was in foul territory. He was outside the line when he dropped the ball," the manager was saying.

"Yes, he was *on* the line but that doesn't matter," I replied. "It's where the ball is when it touches the fielder. And, in my judgment, that ball was fair when it hit his glove." (Remember those three words: "In my judgment.")

"No, no, no. He was on the line. It's foul," the manager continued. He was not understanding my explanation.

I mean, have you ever seen an umpire reverse a call? "Oh, yes, Mr. Manager. You're absolutely correct. I totally blew that call. Thank you for pointing that out to me in front of all these people." Neither have I.

"Sir," I said, doing my best to remain calm, "it doesn't matter where the fielder is standing. It's where the ball is that makes the difference."

"And the ball was on the line. It's foul."

"If the ball was on the line, then it's fair. And this ball was fair. The batter is *out!*" I finally declared with a raised fist indicating the out. I then turned to walk back to the home plate area. Honestly, I wish these guys would just read their rulebook.

It's just for cases like this why the umpire is encouraged to call "Infield Fly, if fair" when the ball is close to the foul line. It avoids as much confusion as possible, as soon as possible, and as emphatically as possible.

* * *

The idea behind the Infield Fly Rule is to avoid a cheap double play, a pop-up in the infield, the runners being on first and second or with the bases loaded would have to wait until the ball is caught or dropped before being able to advance. Without the batter being automatically out, were the fielder allow the ball to drop, the runners would be easy victims of force-outs at second and third. Such is the reasoning behind the Infield Fly Rule.

Unfortunately one third base coach in the seven-to twelve-year-old division didn't understand the rule entirely.

Life Behind The Mask

With one out and the bases full, the batter popped the ball up to the first-base side of the pitcher's mound.

In order to protect the pitcher from potential injury, it's the catcher's job to direct either the first baseman or second baseman to take the catch. Unfortunately not many teams at this age level practice this play and even fewer catchers are aware of their responsibility. In this case, with runners on all the bases, both fielders stayed at their respective corners, leaving the pitcher to make the catch himself.

As the ball came down, I made the call of "Infield fly! Batter is out!"

At that point, the batter is officially out whether the ball is caught or not. If caught, the runners would have to tag up before attempting to advance. This was not a problem as all three runners were staying on their bases waiting to see if they could advance. With a pop-up inside the sixty-foot bases paths, there's usually no advance attempted by the runners. But, in dealing with the younger players, twelve and under, nothing is a given. And this was no exception.

Two developments created total confusion on the bases. First – the batter advanced to first base, unaware of already being called him out despite my loud voice (honestly, these players get in such a zone, they are oblivious to the whole world around them). The second was the pitcher failed to make a clean catch and the ball fell to the ground. Not a problem because the batter was already out, so the other runners did not have to advance even with the ball not being caught.

But the ball on the ground seemed to ignite a fire to the runner on second.

With two outs now recorded, the pitcher quickly recovered the ball and, maybe thinking he needed to throw out this advancing runner, threw to third base. This had the immediate effect of the runner on third heading for home as the runner from second continued toward him. The coach at third was screaming at both runners to get back to their

31

previous bases. Before the lead runner could stop (or so he said afterward), he crossed home plate. In all honesty, he may not have even heard the coach or realized he was shouting at him but the youngster from second base clearly saw the stop sign being thrown up in front of him and, although more than half way to third base, immediately stopped and ran back to second base. Not, however, before the ball beat him there and a tag applied for the third out.

Did the run count as he scored before the third out was made? I attempted to explain the runners were free to advance without having to tag up because the fly ball was not caught, but the batter was still out because of the Infield Fly Rule. One of these years I should hold a one-day workshop for coaches and players to explain the Infield Fly Rule, how to make an appeal, and a few other things apparently never explained. Or, at least, not understood. Problem is most likely fewer than a half dozen people would show up and it would probably be the ones who already understood these things.

For example (and thank goodness I've never needed to explain this in a game situation), as soon as a fly ball is touched by a defensive player, the runners are free to tag up and head for the next base. They do not have to wait for the ball to be caught and contained before advancing. During the 2009 Major League season, I saw a play where, with a runner on first base, the batter hit a line drive back to the pitcher. He did not catch the ball. In fact, he probably never put a glove on the ball for it most likely hit his left shoulder and ricocheted up into the air as a pop-up toward the second baseman. The runner stopped a few strides off first base and waited to see what was going to happen. When the fielder finally caught the ball, it having never touched the ground, for the second out, then and only then did this Big League, professional baseball player decide to return to first base. The second baseman's quick throw beat him there and he became the third out. If this player had touched up as soon as the ball hit the pitcher, he would have been free to advance and probably the fielder would have thrown to first base thinking he had a force-out with the runner very close to second base by that time.

It's just such little things to significantly change the outcome of a ballgame. But how many players, coaches or managers, even in the Bigs, realize these details of the rules? Umpires must know all of these rules and how to apply them at a moment's notice.

* * *

Let me insert a couple of knotty problems here to see if you are on your toes for the call of an infield fly. Situation Number 1: Pop-up fly with no outs and runners on first and second is an infield fly. The ball drops to the ground with no fielder touching it, hits the first base bag and ricochets into foul territory before the base where it strikes the coach in the box. What is the call?

Situation Number 2: Pop-up fly with one out and bases loaded is an infield fly. Hit between the first and second baseman, they collide when both attempt to catch the ball without benefit of calling for it. The ball lands untouched by either infielder, then bounces into right field where the outfielder there picks up the ball and throws it back to the infield. What is the call?

Oh, I'm not going to give you the answers. The whole point of knotty problems is to make you think about the play and the proper call.

* * *

In addition to possessing a common language and understanding of the basics to get through a game, you must also understand the urban legends that are not true and therefore do not apply to the official rules of baseball.

The most significant false statement is "ties go to the runner." If the ball and the runner get to a base at the same time, the runner is safe, right? If I would put it to fifteen umpires, from all venues of baseball, I would certainly hope none would agree with that statement.

This is not which came first, the chicken or the egg, but it is a case of something got there first. One umpire summed it up very easily for me: "In order to be safe, the runner has to beat the throw to the bag. If he didn't beat it, he's out." And once again lest we forget the three most important words in an umpire's vocabulary—"In my judgment."

End of discussion.

Some umpires may tell you they watch the foot reaching the bag and listen for the ball hitting the glove. I strongly disagree with that. My feeling is the umpire needs to be close enough to see the play before him but not so close that he can't see the entire play. If you're so close you can't see when the ball hits the glove, you need to back up a couple of steps. What if the ball smacks into the glove but then pops out again? The umpire who listens for the ball could call the runner out because the ball got there first even if it's then lying on the ground. My brother, Bob, taught me to look at the entire play before making the call. Look and make sure the fielder is clearly holding on to the ball and not trying to contain it. If the runner slid into second base and the fielder had his glove down in front of the runner but now the umpire can't see if the ball is in there or not, he shouldn't be afraid to tell that fielder, "Show me the ball." If that player has to reach down with his bare hand to pick it up off the ground, he probably didn't have control of it during the play, therefore the runner would be safe. If he immediately brings up the glove with the ball firmly in the pocket or webbing, ring that runner up. I seriously had a fielder tell me, "I can't, he's sitting on it," indicating the runner. That man was safe because the fielder did not contain the ball. This is not a game of dodge ball where you try to hit the runner with the ball (although there have been many instances where such is exactly the case). You have to tag him with the ball (even if in your glove) while controlling the spheroid.

Many times in games, I've seen a fielder slap his glove down for a swipe tag only to have the ball fly out of the glove. In those cases, the fielder did not maintain complete control throughout the play and the runner would be safe. Only in the rare cases where an umpire may rule the ball came out of the glove while the fielder was attempting to transfer it to his bare hand could the runner be called out. That's a prime example of an umpire's judgment of the situation. But, as I say, that type of call is very rare.

*   *   *

And that situation brings up another point I had in a ten- and eleven-year-old's game just a few years ago. With a runner on first base and nobody out, the batter was instructed to sacrifice bunt to advance the runner. He laid a beautiful bunt down the first base line.

The first baseman charged and picked up the ball in his bare hand as the batter advanced towards him. As opposed to turning around and throwing the ball to the pitcher covering the bag, this fielder decided to tag the runner himself. However, he reached out with his glove to put a tag on the runner while still holding the ball in his bare hand.

This runner would not have been out because of the empty glove tag. But his own actions caused him to be out. No, he didn't swat at the fielder to avoid the tag or try to dislodge the ball from the player's possession. Rather he moved several steps into foul territory to sidestep the tag. In fact, he moved well more than three feet away to avoid the tag and therefore was out for his own actions. I rang him up. And his coaches went ballistic!

Not only did the offensive coach from first base step forward to argue with me but the coach from the third base box also wanted to get in his two cents. But he went a little too far.

They argued that the fielder has to tag him with the ball

or the ball in the glove. And I wholeheartedly agreed with them. So the third base coach, the manager of the team, told the batter to get on first base even though he hadn't reached that far while the play was still going on. And I repeated that the batter/runner was out. Before I could explain why, the coach was literally in my face to argue the point.

"He tagged him with an empty glove, and you still call him out?"

"That's right."

"He's not out. He's got to be tagged with the ball."

"Generally, I'd agree with you, sir," I said, maintaining my composure while this coach was certainly not controlling his.

"You need to go back to Umpire School, Blue. That's basic Umpiring 101." He was now shouting, not so much at me but to get the bench and spectators on his side and against me. There he crossed the line. I'm all for freedom of speech but when a manager, coach or even a player starts dramatically talking with the spectators or other participants in the game to degrade the umpire or any other participant in the game, such behavior has no place in the game of baseball. Even the rules agree with that one.

I took a step back from him and pointed to the batter/runner standing on first base. "That runner is out!" I shouted for all to hear. I then pointed to the arguing manager, "And you're gone!"

If he had approached me as a gentleman and asked me why I had called the batter out, I would have explained he went more than three feet out of the base path to avoid the tag and was therefore called out. Instead he attempted to show me up to his spectators and didn't see the end of the game.

He did approach me after the game concluded (so obviously he hadn't left the park as he was required and I really couldn't tell you if his team had won or not) to continue his argument. I attempted to put an end to it as

36

quickly as possible by telling him "Your runner went outside the three feet to avoid the tag. *That* is why I called him out."

He considered my words for a moment and even looked over to the first baseline where the event had occurred. "Why didn't you say that then?" he asked.

"Coach," I said calmly, "you never gave me the chance." I concluded with a chuckle and walked away.

*   *   *

Another urban legend of baseball: "Even if the fielder falls into the stands while catching the ball, the batter is still out." This also is an issue of containing the ball. And, again, the umpire shouldn't be afraid to challenge the fielder to show the ball.

If he obviously has the ball caught and contained before he falls into the seats (or, in the case of youth baseball, parents watching the game in folding lawn chairs) and then drops it, the rulebook is quite specific about how to cover that. If the fielder catches the ball and then falls into the seats, the batter is out, the ball is dead and each runner is entitled to advance one base without jeopardy of being put out even if they demonstrated no intention of doing such during the catch. The key is the fielder must contain and control the ball prior to or at least while he is falling into the seats. If he first falls in, then completes the catch, it's a foul ball, out of play. He cannot extend the playing field into the seats. However (here is another one of those exceptions), he may reach or step into the dugout to make a catch as long as he does control and contain the ball. Not only is the catch allowed, the ball is still in play because, surprisingly enough, the dugouts are considered to be part of the playing field and runners may advance at their own peril.

Now, if he catches the ball in the field of play and stays on his feet, even if he then goes entirely into the dugout or spectator area, as long is there isn't interference with the

37

player or the baseball, the ball could be alive and in play (umpire's judgment call). If he either falls down (or is supported by players or spectators to prevent his falling—a judgment call) or then drops the ball after initially containing the ball (also judgment call), the ball is dead, the batter is out and the runners advance no more than one base.

Keep in mind those runners must first retouch their previous base before advancing because the fly ball was caught. If they fail to retouch after the catch and advance that one base while the ball is dead, once it is put back in play, the runner may be called out on appeal for leaving the base too early. We'll deal with proper appeal plays in a bit.

*   *   *

In a nine-and ten-year-old's contest with runners on first and third, the batter popped a fly into foul territory toward but slightly behind first base of a fenceless field. The first baseman glides over towards a group of parents in lawn chairs to catch the foul ball. As the plate umpire, I moved over into foul territory about three steps down and away from the third baseline. My intent was to watch the catch and the runners tagging up all in one vision. My field umpire was there behind first base to judge the catch but I needed to see the tag up as well. Both umpires were in position but the first baseman decided to turn towards the parents with his back to the base umpire. When he made the catch, he promptly fell into the lap of a parent in a chair. "Batter's out," my partner immediately declared. "Dead ball." He pointed to me to complete the call.

"Runners advance one base," I said, noting that both runners maintained contact with their respective bases so tag ups were already made. "Third to home, first to second." I instructed and then repeated, "Dead ball." We both then raised our hands above our heads to indicate to all the ball was dead and the play was done.

We were both on the same page and made the correct

call. There was no Infield Fly Rule because second base was empty and the ball was clearly foul but the call was as smooth as in such case.

The communication, both verbal and non-verbal between umpires, is crucial to demonstrating a command and understanding of the applicable rules and therefore the game before them.

A "G" League contest on Earley's Hill Field #3 in Alliance I remember all too well. With no outs and a runner on first base, the pitcher was heading for his team's bench (no dugouts on this field, only 10" × 2" × 10' planks mounted on three or four pipes sticking out of the ground) in pursuit of a pop-up in foul territory. As he approached the bench, he timed his steps just right that he jumped up on the bench just in time to make the catch and then stood there with the ball firmly held in his glove. Deciding the intent of the rule dealing with dugouts in Major League parks could apply to this situation, I ruled the fielder had legally extended the field onto the bench to make the catch. Therefore the catch was legal. "Batter's out," was the appropriate call but the ball was technically still in play, although no one knew that but me because the runner didn't try to advance and the coach did not encourage him to do so.

Now if he had completed his step on the bench and placed his next foot on the ground behind the bench while completely containing that ball, it would have been a dead ball because being entirely in dead territory and could not legally make the catch. Of course that decision would have been a judgment call.

* * *

Another urban legend is that the batter does not get first base if hit by a pitch that hits the ground first. Believe me with the younger kids, it comes up more times than I can remember and in each case explanations to the managers were necessary.

When a pitched ball strikes (although the rulebook uses the word touches) the batter, one thing is automatic: the ball is dead. As far as the batter being awarded first base, there are several things to consider. The first – location of the baseball when it struck – excuse me – touched the batter. Was it in the strike zone? If so, then it is a strike (no pun intended) and the ball is dead. No runners may advance and the batter continues his turn at bat with the appropriate count. And if such was the third strike, the batter is out and the ball is dead. The second thing to consider – regardless of location, did the batter make any serious effort to get out of the way of the ball? If no discernible effort was made (had time permitted), the pitch is called as the umpire saw it, the ball is dead, no runners may advance, and the batter continues with his turn at bat with the appropriate count.

Now if the pitch was not in the strike zone and the batter made a serious but unsuccessful effort to avoid getting hit (and an umpire must use his judgment to decide if the batter even had time to get out of the way), the batter should be awarded first base and other runners shall advance only if they are forced. No place within that explanation does it mention that the ball must be in flight when it touches the batter or may not have touched the ground before hitting the batter.

Take, for example, a pitch low in the dirt at the batter's feet. Is the umpire supposed to determine if the ball struck the ground before it touched the batter's shoes? From the position squatting behind the catcher, it could be a difficult viewpoint to make such a decision. Granted, if it struck considerably away from the batter and then bounced up to touch his leg, that could be easier to call, but the rules try to be as uniform as possible (except for the numerous exceptions).

Let's try to confuse the matter even more. If a ball thrown by the pitcher from the pitcher's rubber hits the ground and does not proceed far enough to cross the foul line on the field or home plate itself (and please remember the entirety of home plate is within fair territory and therefore before the foul lines) without meeting an obstruction, it shall not be considered a pitch but rather shall be called 'no pitch.' With men on base, this would be a balk and all runners (but not the batter) would advance one base without jeopardy of being put out. Personally, I also include portions of the batter's boxes in that definition because many batters actually stand in advance of the foul line so the ball never crosses the foul lines when they hit it.

Then there is the other side of the call. If the pitched ball hits the ground before reaching home plate but then bounces such that it crosses the plate within the strike zone, it shall be called a ball. To be a strike it must enter a portion of the three-dimensional strike zone in flight. Obviously if the ball hit the ground first, it is not in flight but rather considered a bouncing ball. The same as if a fielder would catch a ball on first bounce it would not be a fly-out because the ball was not in flight but rather a bouncing ball.

Now of course, if the batter swings at the ball, his actions shall have the same effect as if he did so while the ball was in flight. Swing and a miss is still a strike. Swing and hit the ball is still a hit and the ball is alive and in play (unless, of course, it is a foul ball and then it shall be called such).

The pitcher delivers the ball toward home plate but hits the ground before the plate and stops short in the loose dirt before the plate.

In my more than forty years, I have seen three different actions occur following such a pitch. The first is the easiest. Since the ball did not cross the foul line, it's a 'no pitch' and in a division where lead-offs are prohibited, there is no penalty to be associated with such. The rulebook specifies that such an action shall be determined to be no pitch. It does not address the issue of a balk. A balk is a judgment call and is defined as an action by the pitcher while on the rubber meant to deceive a runner. Throwing the ball toward home plate and the batter but not making it past the foul line is not an action to deceive a runner.

In the second, I have seen the catcher quickly reach forward to pick up the ball, perhaps before the umpire had a chance to determine if indeed it had completely stopped. The result is the umpire must then rule either the ball did stop and is therefore no pitch (the easiest determination in the lower divisions of play) or that the catcher interfered with the batter's opportunity to offer at the ball. Such interference would result in the batter being awarded first base and any runner who is forced to advance would be entitled to do so one base without peril of being put out. Remember, though, if the catcher reaches onto the field of play to pick up a ball that had not crossed the foul lines and the batter makes no action to swing at the ball, it shall be called a no pitch and is a dead ball. No wonder people are confused by the rules.

The third possible scenario, and this I have seen happen, is the batter takes a swing at the ball lying there before the plate. If he hits it, he cannot have either foot completely on the ground outside of the batter's box when he makes contact or he shall be declared out. If the batter hits the ball cleanly and fairly, then run, batter, run. You treat it like a regular hit, as if he struck the ball while in flight.

And I have seen all three scenarios. Probably harder than knowing the right call to make in each situation is doing your best to keep a straight face at the batter who has just golfed the ball over the shortstop's head into left field. I have seen some batters do better with their aluminum bats than I can do with my sand wedge. It can be discouraging at times, but mostly it is humorous. And that is just one of the numerous reasons why I love this level of play.

* * *

Somewhere within the mystery of unschooled baseball

rules someone taught, in order to make an appeal on a runner, the ball must first go back to the pitcher. This is an urban legend to the max and adds to the confusion surrounding how to make an appeal. The appeal play is probably the hardest for the youngest players to understand. Many managers don't comprehend it either. Even the Big Boys err when attempting an appeal play.

The first thing to remember is the ball must be in play. Do not call (actually asked for) "Time out!" All too often managers see a runner missed the base (for those managers who actually watch the opposing team's runners) and can get an easy out if only he had practiced how to make an appeal with his players. The first thing the manager shouts to his players is, "Get the ball to the pitcher."

The ball does not have to go back to the pitcher first to make an appeal.

Example: with a runner on first base, the batter sends a deep drive to right field. The right fielder catches the ball, but the runner took off before the catch was made. The throw is into the first baseman and the manager is shouting at him to get the ball to the pitcher. However, the first baseman can just walk over to the bag with the ball in his control and step on the base while explaining to the umpire the runner left early. If the umpire saw it happen that way, he can call the runner out right then. The ball is still in play and, if there had been a runner on second or third and was now trying to score, a throw to the plate could result in a triple play. Even, let's say the first baseman received the throw from the right fielder and threw to home in time to get the runner trying to score. Without going to the pitcher, the catcher could throw the ball back to the first baseman (or anyone covering first, for that matter) to make the same appeal. It's not that a play occurred before the appeal making it void. The whole thing is one continuous play. (I know I explained elsewhere that a similar play was actually three different plays but that was when considering whether or not to count a run scored during the same play as the third out. Comparing that play to this is like comparing apples to applesauce: kind of the same but only different. I told you this umpiring thing is confusing!)

I know I'm opening a can of worms with this section but I believe, in addition to presenting several humorous stories, it is also an opportunity to provide some instruction.

A few nights ago in a ten-to twelve-year-old's contest, with a runner on second base and only one out, the batter lifted a short fly ball into right field. The ball was obviously going to fall safely so the runner took off for third base with visions of scoring as the batter/runner would distract the defensive players on the other side of the infield. However, when he made his big turn at third base, he failed to touch the base. His miss was very evident to everyone at the field but he made no effort to go back before crossing home plate and heading for the dugout. Maybe he thought if he got into the dugout everything would be okay.

The defensive manager screamed at his players to get the ball back to the pitcher. With the batter/runner standing on first base, the ball was returned to the pitcher who then asked for time. Wrong move, son. Time was granted. He then threw the ball over to the third baseman standing on the bag. Neither my umpiring partner in the field or I made any call. The defensive manager then instructed his third baseman to tell the umpires he was making an appeal. Once that announcement was made, from home plate I responded, "Time has been called. The ball must be in play to make an appeal."

The dejected manager hung his head as the ball went back to the pitcher. Here he had a perfect out play because the runner was prohibited from returning to the field to correct his error, having already entered the dugout and thereby terminating his participation in the play on the field. All they had to do was conduct a proper appeal play and they could get the second out of the inning. But, they blew it. It was only a temporary error because, once the ball was back in play, they could conduct a proper appeal.

The pitcher accepted the ball and, with the next batter ready for the pitch, he stepped on the rubber and I called, "Play ball!" My umpiring partner and I were expecting him to step off and again throw to third base for the proper appeal. So much so that I really wasn't set behind the catcher as I would normally be for a pitch. This pitcher went into a short wind-up and threw to the plate thus ending any hope of an appeal play.

We found out later that the manager thought, with the improper appeal, he'd lost the opportunity to make an appeal. His reasoning was the unsuccessful appeal was considered a play and voided any attempt at a second appeal. My umpiring partner and I explained to him the attempt while the ball was dead, while time was called, is not considered a play and therefore he could have still made the appeal once the ball was put back into play. "Why didn't you tell me that then?" the manager asked.

"We can't provide instructions like that during the game," we explained. "It would be giving an unfair advantage to one team over the other." And, of course, no manager would want that, right?

*   *   *

If the ball does go back to the pitcher for the appeal, it becomes very important that he steps off from the rubber before throwing the ball to the appropriate base for an appeal.

In a thirteen-and fourteen-year-old division game, following a fly out to right field with runners previously on second and third, now being two outs, both runners scored as the right fielder held the ball, not sure where to throw. The runner on third is thought to have left early by the defensive team. The ball went back to the pitcher and, while standing on the rubber with the next batter in the box, threw to third base for an appeal. By rule he threw to an unoccupied base and committed a balk. Yes, I said the pitcher balked with no runners on base. Because he stood on the rubber while throwing to an unoccupied base, the rules view it was a balk even though he was obviously attempting to pick off a runner who left early.

Therefore, in the intention of the pitcher, there was still a runner on third base, a runner he was trying to put out. But he still had his foot on the rubber when he threw to the base. That became his mistake. And, because he balked while trying to make an appeal, that effort is considered to be a play and no further attempts at an appeal shall be recognized.

If the ball comes back to the pitcher to start the appeal, he must not start a windup or come to the set position. Such, too, could be interpreted as a play and not as part of the appeal process. Even tossing the ball up and down while standing on the rubber waiting for a fielder to get in position is a balk because he is throwing the ball to some place other than home plate or a base. A balk is a play and a play therefore prohibits a subsequent appeal play.

He should promptly disengage from the rubber, announce his intent to make an appeal and then throw directly and without hesitation to the base where the appeal is to be made. Admittedly there are instances where the pitcher must step onto the rubber to institute an appeal. If, for some reason, time were called following a play where a runner is suspected of leaving early or missing a base or passing a preceding runner, the ball must be put back into play before starting the appeal.

After putting the ball in play, the pitcher needs to immediately step off the back of the rubber toward second base (for a move to any other direction could be viewed as a motion to another base and could create a balk situation) and then continue with the appeal process.

With a hand on the Bible, I swear this happened. The

runner on second was thought to have left early but advanced only to third base. The ball came back to the pitcher and he announced the appeal. The third base coach then told the runner to get back on second base. As he broke for second (he is allowed to run the bases in reverse order if attempting to retouch a missed base or if he left early following a legal catch), the pitcher stopped in his motion of throwing to the second baseman covering the bag and then threw instead to the shortstop who was closest to the returning runner. The result of the rundown found the runner standing back on third base while still never retouching second base. The ball was returned to the pitcher and he started the process all over again. Except then it was invalid because the unsuccessful rundown resulted as a play being made before the appeal. While the pitcher threw to second base, the heads up coach then told the runner to head for home. With the ball firmly in the glove of the second baseman and his foot appropriately on the base for the appeal, the runner was called safe as he crossed home plate. I made no friends on the defensive team with that call but, following the game, I took the time to work with the manager and his players on how to properly make an appeal play and they were then appreciative of the call and my effort to correct them.

*   *   *

While I'm discussing appeal plays, let's just examine what is probably the hardest area to explain. And, believe me, I have had to do it more than once on the field.

When a caught foul ball is such that the fielder's effort to make the catch takes him and the ball out of the field of play, the ball is dead and all runners advance no more than one base without peril. They first, however, must tag up at the base they were standing prior to the pitch being made.

In a high school level game, runners on first and third with one out, the batter popped up the ball toward his team's dugout (and, yes, this particular field actually had dugouts on the sides of the field). Both runners advanced about a third of the way down the lines as the catcher ran over to the dugout to make the catch. The pitcher, however, did not come in to cover home plate with the runner on third base, as he should have. It turned out not to be a factor but I just mention it to place the fielder.

The home plate umpire moved over with the catcher as I (field umpire) maintained the outside "C" position to watch the timing of the catch and the runners tagging up. As the catcher neared the dugout and it became obvious he must enter the area to make the catch, the offensive team's players in the dugout all backed up to give him room but no one stepped forward to catch him if he tumbled into the dugout. (That's a Catch-22 because when does attempting to support the opposing team's catcher become interfering with his effort to catch the ball and make an out? So most teams will give ground and let him fall.)

He successfully caught the ball with one foot on the dugout steps and the other in mid-air before crashing into the dugout. My umpiring partner signals a good catch and the batter is out and then declares the ball is dead because of the catcher falling into the dugout. Both runners may advance one base.

As the catch become imminent, the runner on third had returned to the bag to tag up and score so he was good to advance to home plate for his one base. The runner on first, however, began a slow trot to second base without first returning to first for the tag up. Once he reached second base, whether trying to be helpful or not I'm not sure, the shortstop tells the runner, "Ah, you didn't tag up."

"I don't need to," he said. "The umpire told me to advance one base. So here I am."

The shortstop looks at me for confirmation. I really can't say anything so as not to give an unfair advantage so I raised my hands as if to say, "Don't ask me."

The ball went back to the pitcher but was still not in play

when the shortstop trotted over to the mound to tell his teammate something. Once the pitcher put the ball back into play, he stepped off the back of the pitching rubber and threw over to first base. "Runner didn't tag up after the pop-out," he tells me.

I repeated. "Runner didn't tag up. He is out. That was the third out of the inning and the run does not count."

"What do you mean I'm out?" challenged this more than six-foot tall player (I stand only five-ten). "He told me to go to second," he said, indicating the home plate umpire.

The defensive team was leaving the field, having retired three opponents in the half-inning but this player remained to argue with me. "Yes, he did tell you to go to second but you know when there is a fly ball caught for an out, the runners have to tag up before advancing."

"He didn't say anything about that," this youngster argued as his teammates came onto the field to play defense.

"C'mon, Paul, you know he's right," offered the center fielder as he crossed the field to his defensive position. "Get your glove and let's beat these turkeys." And for some reason this player was more willing to follow the suggestion of his teammate than the umpire telling him he was out.

When a fly ball is caught, even if the fielder then falls into dead territory or something occurs making the ball dead, the runners still must tag up before advancing for an awarded base.

*   *   *

The other side of the coin is a successful appeal play.

Little League plays six-inning games so when we started the eighth inning it had already become a long night. In the top of the eighth, the visiting team was able to score two runs. So obviously in the bottom of the inning the home team knew they needed at least two runs to keep playing but would have preferred three to win the game and go home.

The first batter sent a dribbler to the shortstop for out number one. The second batter worked the pitcher to a full count, fouling off at least five pitches before swinging at ball four for the second out. In Little League a pitcher can throw only a certain number of pitches depending on his age. This pitcher reached his limit and the fifth pitcher of the night was brought in. Not too many teams actually have five pitchers and this was no exception. The next batter was hit by the third pitch and went to first base. The next batter smashed a line drive past the second baseman and left runners on first and third with two outs.

With two outs already in the inning, the pitcher attempted to get a strikeout to close the game. Unfortunately, the third pitch was lifted into right field and over the fence for the game-winning home run … except after all the dust had cleared, the defensive team was still on the field at the insistence of their manager. The manager walked out to me behind home plate and said, "The first runner missed home plate." And he was right (but I couldn't admit that to him). "You need to make an appeal but, because the ball was hit out of play, it must be put back into play first."

"How do we do that when the game is over?" he asked.

"You've kept your players on the field," I observed. "That's a good thing. Your pitcher needs to put the ball in play," I stated while taking another ball out from the ball bag on my hip, "and make a proper appeal to home plate."

"How does he do that?" was the next question.

"Oh, I can't tell you that," I impartially told him with a chuckle, "but you've practiced appeal plays, right?"

Very few teams do and this was no exception.

"Okay, at least give it a try."

I tossed the ball out to the pitcher and indicated to the bench of the winning team, "I need a batter up here."

"What for?" was the honest response. "The game is

over."

Not being able to give instructions to either team, I couldn't explain why I was doing this, so I gave the command, "Batter up." No one from the offensive team approached the plate.

In fact they were packing up their equipment, so I shouted the instruction a second time and then indicated for the pitcher to toe the rubber before saying, "Play ball."

As the offensive team stopped what they were doing to watch the post-game show on the field, the pitcher properly stepped back off the rubber as the catcher stepped well away from home plate to accept the thrown ball from the pitcher. He then walked back to me and said, "The first runner missed home plate." I looked down to see that the catcher's foot was coincidentally on home plate. My reaction brought shouts from both sides of the field. One side was glee while the other was far from it.

"The first runner missed home plate," I shouted for all to hear. "He is out by appeal. His was the third out of the inning. No runs score and we are done."

There was a considerable time of explanation and instruction following this one but, in the end, everyone understood what had happened and why. At least I hope everyone understood. The lessons learned here: it is very important for the runners to make sure and touch all the bases (even sometimes the big boys miss a few). It is also important that someone from the defensive team watches those runners and knows what to do if they miss a base. And it is absolutely imperative for the umpires to watch everything on the field because you never know when it may come back at you.

"Let's Play Ball!"

In the Major Leagues, the umpiring crew starts the game with at least four dozen new baseballs prepared for the game. In the youth baseball leagues that number is two new baseballs, maybe three. And these are generally given to the umpire still in the plastic pouch to confirm nothing's been done to them prior to the umpire receiving them, usually at home plate during the ground rules meeting. So, when a pitch is fouled off into the bleachers or hit over the fence for a home run, it is imperative the ball be returned to the umpire as soon as possible.

And it never fails when a batter fouls off one pitch, he is going to foul off a few more. Most times they stay within the fenced playing field, but not all fields are completely enclosed by fences. In fact I have played at fields where there were no fences and two fields would share some of the outfield area.

My favorite field in Alliance, known as Regina Coeli #2 for the Catholic Church and school that owned the property of the two baseball field park. Being located in a growing residential area of town, these fields were small. The left field of field # 2 shared about twelve yards of depth with the right field for field #1. When I had the ten-year-old and under boys on field #2 and the eleven-and twelve-year-old division played on field #1, it was not unusual for us to have to call time for a long ball hit into our outfield. On more than one occasion, the ball rolled all the way through the outfield and into the infield area of field #2. Doubtless it was a home run but, with no fence to determine that distance, the defensive player would have to recover the ball and throw it back to his own field. Admittedly more than once, one of the younger players would pick up the ball to give it to the player coming to retrieve it for his game. This action of intended courtesy would infuriate the player because he felt he could get the ball quick enough to nail the batter/runner at third base but instead he usually got a home run because of the interference. I finally had to add to my ground rule instructions, they should leave the ball alone so the other players could field it. And I have been on both sides of the play where I have been working a game on Regina Coeli #1 and had to award that home run because someone picked up the ball to help.

Another feature of this facility was located no more than seven yards behind the backstop on field #2 (a backstop, I should note, having no top-over section to contain the foul balls). A wooded area of maybe twenty-five or thirty yards in depth acted as a buffer zone between the park and a residential sub-division. Within these woods were various hazards, some a nature trail wouldn't tolerate – a storm creek for rain water runoff, numerous small animals who built homes in the ground or around fallen trees (and sometimes come out to the edge of the woods to watch the game), several dramatic changes in elevation of the ground of about four feet within an eight-foot distance. And my least favorite thing of all – a patch of poison ivy that acted like a magnet for the foul balls. And this is one umpire who is *very allergic to poison ivy.*

The ball would land in the patch and be returned to me without being wiped off first. I would dump it in my ball bag on my right hip or in my pants pocket if I didn't have the pouch on that evening and continue with the game. Inside my ball bag was built in a towel where I could wipe off the ball before throwing it out the pitcher when needed. Obviously the pants pocket didn't have such a feature. Either way the poison ivy juices were on my hand from receiving the ball during the course of a game, this umpire sweats. For at least one season, I spent the entire summer with poison ivy from chest to knees and every (and I mean *every*) inch between.

If you are not allergic to poison ivy, and apparently few of the numerous players on that field throughout the years were, you have no idea how much it itches and you *can't scratch.* I practically lived in the pink calamine lotion one summer, so much so, I didn't need sunscreen. And, yes, I washed the ball bag in hot water by itself before going through the laundry after every game, which is why it wasn't always available for the next game. I have been told that the sap (venom?) from poison ivy can linger in clothing for more than a year and I could believe that.

I have been to the hospital emergency room more than once for the poison ivy but one thing I did discover: other people close to me are no, not so much as a bump. Me, however, you could play connect the dots with a fine tip pen. And I never heard of a pitcher complaining about poison ivy so I have to think the idea of the towel sewn into the ball pouch worked – at least for them.

*   *   *

This is youth baseball, played on community fields maintained by the local park and recreation boards with the assistance of volunteers. There are bound to be unusual conditions for the baseball field. In Ohio, when it rained during the day, quite frequently games were canceled because the fields were not designed for runoff and the dirt infields would hold the water, especially around the bases. It could be pouring rain in the south end of town around Butler-Rodman Park but not have a drop of rain at Earley's Hill Park in the northern end of town. So parents, coaches and umpires would have to listen to the five o'clock news on the local radio station for information of whether games were being played that evening.

The fields were designed such that the pitcher's mounds were actually level ground so there were valleys directly in front of the rubber and another where the pitcher would land his throwing foot. Generally speaking the city crews came out in the afternoon to drag the fields, then mark the base paths and batter's boxes with powdered chalk or lime. If it rained after that, any further maintenance was up to the managers of the teams.

As a rule, umpires were not permitted to assist in preparing the fields for play. Should any player get injured during the game because of something we, as appointed and paid representatives of the league, had done, it could become an issue of legal responsibility. I did keep a bag of sand and a garden rake in the trunk of my car for managers to use in filling in water puddles around the home plate area and elsewhere on the field.

One summer, a local sawmill decided to donate its sawdust to the city for use at the fields to absorb the water around the bases and at home plate. This was a wonderful idea as it usually cost the park and recreation board several thousand dollars over the course of the summer to purchase sand and dirt for the dozen or so baseball fields. Doubtlessly it also worked out well for the sawmill, not having to have pay to haul away the sawdust from their facility. So it was a win-win situation for everybody. Right?

As is to be expected, no good deed goes unpunished. The sawdust was very absorbent and, although it would clump together and sometimes get stuck in the bottoms of players' shoes, it worked out well. That is until we started finding ground up pieces of nails around the bases and at home plate about three weeks into the summer. Apparently someone at the sawmill ran some used boards through the grinder without first removing the nails. This resulted in small pieces of metal mixed in with the sawdust. After the adult managers, coaches and even this umpire picked through the sawdust to the best of our abilities before starting the game, the players were still finding small nail pieces during the contest. Thankfully no one was injured but it made everyone leery of sliding into a base.

The mayor soon received many phone calls on this issue and the free sawdust ended for the summer. The fields were dragged and, as best as possible, the sawdust, etc. removed.

File this one under "it seemed like a good idea at the

time."

*   *   *

Another feature of these municipal fields was that some had chain link fences surrounding them in an effort to keep the ball within the playing field. Over the many years these fences would become damaged by vandals or with holes dug under them by stray animals getting from point A to point B by the shortest possible path. So it became necessary to make special ground rules for balls stuck under or even into the fences and backstop. For the outfield fences the rule was if the ball rolls under or through the fence or gets stuck, the outfielder should turn to the umpire and raise his hands in the air to indicate there is a problem. The umpire then would run out to the player and verify that the ball was indeed stuck or whatever. The runners would then be placed where in the umpire's judgment they would have obtained by the ground rule double.

That worked out well as the boys were, for the most part, honest about not being able to get to the ball. Until . . .

In a "G" League contest in Akron (players eleven-and twelve-years-old), with runners on first and second, the batter lifted a fly ball over the center fielder's head but not over the fence. As the fielder ran back toward the fence, I, as the only umpire assigned to the contest, was staying in foul ground between third and home plate for the potential play at either base. Taking note of where the runners had advanced, I was anticipating what was to happen. Sure enough the center fielder reached the fence and then raised his hands over his head to indicate the ball was under the barrier. I started out at a brisk trot to verify that the ball was trapped.

At about the point where I hit the outfield grass behind second base, I could see the player was kicking about with his feet to free the ball and finally succeeded. As I came to a stop and motioned with my hand the ball was free and the runners could advance, he picked up the ball and threw a line drive to home plate to get the runner originally on first now coming in from third base. And I was standing in the area of second base with full gear that included one of those balloon chest protectors, I had absolutely no hope of even being within a hundred feet of the close play at the plate.

Thinking fast, I held up my hands and shouted "Dead ball" and then pointed to runner approaching home plate. "He gets home." Without waiting for any arguments, I turned back to the center fielder and shouted to him, "If you said the ball was stuck under then fence, you shouldn't have been trying to kick it free. You're supposed to leave it alone so I can verify where it is." I pointed back to the home plate area. "That is the penalty for kicking it loose before I got there."

Again, without waiting for the argument from the fielder, I pointed at the batter/runner stopped on first base when I started out to the outfield. "Second base" I granted him for the ground rule double and then turned heel to return to home plate to dust off the base.

Taking the ball from the catcher, I examined it for any cuts or marks from its being stuck under the fence and then kicked loose. All the while I was doing this, my heart raced a hundred miles an hour just waiting for the manager to come out and give me whatever for making up a new rule during the game. But the argument never came. Instead, he shouted out to the center fielder, "Now, if the ball is stuck again, leave it alone 'til the umpire gets there." He agreed with me. I was vindicated! It was logical, and necessary and, most of all, it worked.

Thereafter, I included the instruction of leaving the ball alone once you've raised your hands in the ground rules meetings: "If you're kicking at it while I'm coming out there, I'm going head back for home plate and let the runners go." No one's objected … thank the baseball gods.

* * *

There was another field in Alliance that I was particularly fond of the ground rules made necessary by the environment. Earley's Hill #4 had several huge maple trees behind the first base bench. I have absolutely no idea how old these trees were but they had grown to hang over the bench area and somewhat over the field of play area directly in front of the bench, although all in foul territory. The fields have since been reconfigured so this is no longer a problem. In fact, the trees may have been removed. But, while they were there, as part of the ground rules, a foul ball into the trees was a dead ball and no runners could advance.

In order to protect the players from getting hit on the head or worse from the dropping ball as it ricocheted around in the branches in the trees, I would occasionally call the ball dead before it got to the trees and then the wind would cause it to not get in the trees at all. I explained in ground rules with the managers, "If I call the dead ball in the trees, whether or not it then hits the trees, it is still a dead ball. I'd rather err on the side of caution for the players." It happened several times and I heard about it from managers that, by calling the ball too soon, I was taking the opportunity of making the play away from his fielders. There were valid arguments on both sides of the issue but mine won out because I was wearing the blue shirt. I did learn to delay that call a little bit longer but always made it for the safety of the players.

*   *   *

Then there was the city that did nothing for the fields because of the potential liability. Their legal department had determined that if they did nothing in the maintenance and preparation of the fields, then they could not be blamed for any injuries that might occur during the game. They would cut the grass about once a week but that was it. And it wasn't necessarily mulched, either, so the dead cut grass would accumulate in the outfield to be disturbed only by the wind and the parents who would come out with lawn rakes to clean the field. Instead of field maintenance, they had a pile of sand at each of the fields and a locker where spades and rakes were kept for the managers and parents to tend to the fields themselves. There were also bags of white lime and a spreader for someone to mark the base paths and batter's boxes. It was my sincere hope the youth athletic board did not have to pay the city for the usage of their fields in that community. Of course, I could see the beauty of this situation from the city's perspective. If the parents and the league were willing to accept this condition, it was definitely a win-win situation for the city.

The only potential down side of this was to the umpire who would occasionally have to make special ground rules. There was the issue of the high weeds that would grow around the backstop fencing and, of course, the stubborn water puddles that would not be absorbed no matter how much sand was put into them. On at least one occasion, it became necessary to tell the managers at pre-game meeting "now if the ball goes into the puddle in the first base coach's box, it's a 'Dead Ball' and runners may not advance. And, oh yes, we'll need another ball to use for the rest of the game."

The Alpha and Omega of a Baseball Game

Schedules are drawn up well in advance of the first pitch of the season and in some cases before the leadership of the chapter knows how many teams there are going to be that summer. There is a master list of teams by number, the fields that are available and the dates for the contests drawn up in February for the leagues that begin playing ball in May.

If a chapter has sixteen "H" league teams, Schedule "A" will be used. Another number of teams are plugged into a different schedule. Very easy, very well organized and everything is planned in advance.

And, please keep in mind the people that do all of this work are volunteers. They don't get paid one red cent for all the work they put into this. It's for the kids. Seems simple enough. How could anything go wrong with such a procedure? Well, there is one uncontrollable force to deal with when scheduling baseball games, especially in Ohio: the weather. Weeknight games usually began at 6 o'clock. As an umpire, I like to get to the field about 5:30 for a couple of reasons. The first is to check the condition of the field to determine if it is playable. If there had been a rainstorm during the day and the field wasn't even marked off, generally that was a good indication that we weren't playing that evening. If there was standing water on the field or if the outfield looked like a rice paddy, it was a good indication that we weren't playing that evening. If I could see the managers and parents with rakes and bags of sand already out on the field when I arrived, that was a good indication they knew I'd have postponed the game so they were going the extra effort to get the field ready.

Now, I'm not saying I am strict on the condition of the field. I am just being mindful of the safety of the players. The last thing I want to have happen is for a player to get injured because of field conditions.

The second reason I like to get to the fields early is to verify for myself that both teams have had the opportunity of conducting infield practice in order for the players to learn the bounces of the field. I'm not sure how many teams actually used

60

that opportunity for that reason, but that's why I felt it was needed.

The rules state the decision or not whether to play the game because of field conditions is up to the home team manager until both managers present the umpire with their line-up cards at home plate. Once the line-up cards were presented, the game was mine to call.

I've had managers short of players at the field, try to use their authority to cancel a game on a perfectly dry field saying it was unplayable. Technically the manager would be within his rights. But I could pretty much guarantee the league president or division commissioner would have a few choice words to say to him at the weekly managers' meeting. Usually we would wait for ten minutes or so for his additional players to show up. But there was this one night that the visiting team manager had something to say before handing over his lineup card. This was at a field in another town his team had to travel to play. The team was unfamiliar to me and he may not have ever played on the field before so his questions could have been valid. He started asking about this condition and that ground rule and why we didn't have fencing behind first and third base to keep the balls in the field. I let him go for a minute or two before I stopped him. "Coach," I finally interrupted, "how many players you got here tonight?" A look over to his bench showed a lot of empty seats.

"We've got seven here now," he answered while looking out towards the parking lot, "but we've got two more on the way. They'll be here by the time we reach them in the batting order."

"You've got them on the starting roster and they're not even here?" I asked as I looked over his batting order. The home manager was confused also.

"What if you get three outs and those players are still not here?" the home manager asked.

According to the youth baseball rulebook, you can start a game with only eight players. If a ninth player didn't arrive by the time his spot in the batting order was reached, it was an automatic out. And every time thereafter until he arrived, an out would be recorded. It could become a real rally killer later in a game. On the field, the team would usually play with only two outfielders and maybe have either the second baseman or shortstop play a little deeper than usual. However, starting with seven is not enough. I had to tell the visiting manager we couldn't start the game until at least one more player was physically at the field. I also reminded him that he had until 6:15 to present a team for play. It was 6:03.

The home manager, who had already put his players on the field, brought them back into the dugout while we waited for the absent player or players. My fear was that since I didn't know this team, the visiting manager could present any youngster as an absent player and neither the home manager or I could really challenge it. It was a point I set my mind about trying to solve while we waited.

At about 6:10 a boy in the uniform of the visiting team (or at least the shirt) arrived in the dugout. I really didn't see where he came from but I didn't believe it was from the parking lot. "We've got eight," the manager shouted out to me at home plate.

Trying to remain calm, I needed to formulate a plan. "Send him out to me, please," I instructed.

He did as I said and this young boy with fielding glove on his hand ready to go walked out to meet me. But so did the manager.

"No, sir," I said. "Just the player, if you please." I was trying to be a cordial as possible to this manager.

They both stopped. "Why just him?" the manager asked while he placed his hand in front of the young boy to stop him from going any farther.

I looked at my watch. It was 6:12. "Sir, you've got three minutes to field a team. I need to speak with your player. Alone, please." I told him. "Your choice."

He leaned over as if to tell the player something. "Coach," I interrupted, taking a few steps closer to them, "now or never. I need that player over here. Not another word said to him."

"Just a moment, Blue," he responded and began to direct the player back to the dugout. As far as I was concerned, this game was done. I walked over to the home manager. "I have the sneaking suspicion that young boy is not on his roster," I told him.

"How do you know?" he asked. "Have you had this team before?"

"No, but for some reason he didn't want me to talk with that player alone so I could compare the name he would give me to one on the roster." I responded while looking at my watch again.

"Smart move, Blue," acknowledged the home manager.

After another minute and with no additional players arriving for the visiting team, I declared the game forfeit and awarded a victory to the home team. The visiting manager did not object. I had called his bluff and he blinked.

In addition to reporting the forfeit to the league president and the Umpire-In-Chief, I also informed him of the incident with the strange player. I don't know if I was right or not, but in my mind I prevented a potentially ineligible youngster from taking the field. Would that single player have helped the visiting team win the game? I'll never know, but that visiting manager's behavior caused his boys to lose it.

* * *

In youth baseball, we start a game with as few as two baseballs so, when one is either hit foul or over the fence or if a ball is accidentally thrown out of play, it is imperative to have it returned to the field as quickly as possible and put in the control of the umpire. After doing this for so many years, few things make me as nervous as when I see a coach at either first or third with a baseball in his hand or pocket or, worse yet, bouncing it up and down in his hand while the legal ball is in play.

With a runner on first in this nine-and ten-year-old division game at Earley's Hill #5, a field with no fences to contain fouled and overthrown baseballs, a recently hit foul ball was tossed out to the coach at first. I could see this out of the corner of my eye as I was in the set position behind home plate and my stomach started to churn at all the possibilities that could happen beginning with he doesn't catch it and it goes onto the field of play while I would have a play going. The easiest way to prevent this would have been to call time but, because the pitcher was already in his motion to the plate, I really didn't feel I should do that, so I let the pitch be thrown and hope for the best.

Never hope for the best because that almost guarantees the worst possible option will happen and probably the one you hadn't considered before. The coach did catch the ball but the catcher didn't stop the pitch. Maybe he cheated a peek out of the

63

corner of his eye at the extra ball on or at least near the field, but the pitched ball skipped right by him and to the backstop, being about ten to fifteen feet behind home plate on this particular field. What happened next, I seriously still have nightmares about!

The runner on the base at first wasn't aware the pitched ball had gotten loose and was nonchalantly returning to the base. The coach, with the returned ball in his hand, was shouting to the runner no more than seven feet away from him, "He dropped the ball! Go to second! Go to second!" He was motioning with his arms where second base was as if clarifying for the runner where he was supposed to run. And, of course, it happened. One of his arm waves occurred when the coach didn't have a firm grip on the ball and it came loose in the general direction of second base but maybe only eight to ten feet along the sixty-foot long base path. Just then the catcher retrieved the errant ball from the backstop and, seeing the runner was still in the area of first base, decided to throw there. Or at least in that general vicinity.

What happened? Yep, you guessed it. The first baseman did not field the throw cleanly and the ball squirted off in the area of the extra ball on the field. As I moved out from behind the plate with my big balloon chest protector in hand toward a spot near the pitching mound, setting up between first and second bases while trying to keep my eye on which ball was which, the fielder turned his back to me to pick up a ball as the runner was trying for second. But which ball did he pick up?

There was still one ball on the ground, very close to this fielder. So close, in fact, that when he took a slide step to throw to second, he kicked the second ball toward the pitcher and me.

I had to keep my eyes on the play but still was able to extend my foot to stop the rolling baseball on the field. The runner at second was out as his attempt to slide into the base under the tag was about a foot short of the base. Before I called him out, I shouted, "I've got time" and emphatically threw up both of my hands. I then reached down and picked up the ball at my feet hoping there would be some way of determining which was the official ball and which was the one just retrieved from foul territory.

The coach tried to say he was sorry, but it didn't help me any.

Life Behind The Mask

I indicated to the second baseman that I needed to see the ball he was holding and he complied. It must have been comical to see the umpire standing in the infield holding a baseball in each hand and looking at them as if expecting them to talk to him. Mark Fidrich I'm not but I probably said something like, "Well, okay guys, give me a clue. Which is which?" Finally I decided.

Placing both balls in the bag on my hip, I announced my decision. "We've got a dead ball when it got away from the catcher," I said pointing back to the home plate area. Then, directing my attention to the youngster standing on second base. "Runner goes back to first."

Then, to the spectators in general, I added, "And, people, please don't throw a ball back on the field when we have a play going on. Wait till I call time and then get the ball back to me, please. Thank you." Always remember your manners. If nothing else, it may be good for a chuckle and could bring the point home stronger.

*   *   *

"Play ball!" They are the two words that excite even the youngest of baseball players and the oldest of fans. It has the equivalent effect as a race car enthusiast hearing, "Gentlemen, start your engines." It's fireworks and explosions, the dropping of the puck at a hockey game, or tossing the basketball in the air for the opening tip-off. Every player has been looking forward to hearing those two words for the past several hours. Except on one occasion.

In preparation for the start of the game, the pitcher is permitted eight pitches or up to one minute for warm-ups. Often times I let it extend beyond that before telling the catcher to throw the ball down to second base. ("Coming down" is the call to alert the fielders to throw in their warm-up balls and get ready for the throw.) Then I'll clean the plate one more time and call the instruction "Batter up" while I walk behind the catcher and adjust my mask. A look around the field and arm motion of acknowledgment to the first and third base coaches and then a quick count of the fielders to make sure we have pitcher, catcher and seven fielders (no more, no less) before pointing to the pitcher and making the call of "Play ba..." The right fielder isn't paying attention. He is watching a butterfly that has just landed on the ground before him. He's even gotten down on his knees to get a closer view.

"Hey, right fielder. You ready to go?" I shouted out to the distracted player. No response, no acknowledgment. He was intently studying this butterfly. Now I wouldn't know a monarch from a tortoiseshell but that didn't matter to this player. Turning to the player's bench, I shouted to the coach, "Is he gonna play this game?" The reaction was a shrug. Apparently he'd seen it before. I pointed to the first baseman and indicated to him to go out and get the boy's attention. As he started out, a spectator shouted from the bleachers, "Let the boy study his lepidopterology for a moment."

Lepidopterology, apparently, is the study of butterflies. At least I hoped it was. And this spectator was apparently the boy's parent. How else would he know such a word? It was at that moment that the butterfly took flight and headed off in the direction of Carolina or some such place. The right fielder stood up, pounded his fist into this glove and set himself in baseball ready position as if nothing unordinary had happened. Now I could declare, "Play ball!" Butterfly class was over and it was time to get down to business.

"Dead Ball" Is the *Pause* Feature of Baseball

Numerous times during the course of a game, the umpire has to put the ball back into play. Technically every time the pitch is fouled off (hit into foul territory), it is out of play and must be put back into play (except when a foul tip is caught and contained by the catcher; we'll be getting into many other exceptions elsewhere). In the youth leagues generally either a fielder or coach will retrieve the foul ball and toss it back to the pitcher who then just gets ready for his next pitch. As I pointed out before, unlike the Major Leagues, we have only two new baseballs to start the game and the umpires have to keep those in play as much as possible. If a ball gets overly soiled or scuffed, it may be withheld from play and possibly a third new ball (or newer ball) may be substituted.

But once the ball has been returned to the pitcher, I know many umpires will just let that action alone place the ball back into play. However, early in my umpiring career I had an instance in a nine-and ten-year-old's contest where the ball was tossed back to the pitcher and he was ready to throw but the batter was looking intently down to his third base coach for the signal. The batter is supposed to step back and put at least one foot out of the batter's box to indicate that he is not ready for the pitch. In this case it appeared the young man had been told by a coach during a previous at-bat to stay in the box. Many players develop a bad habit of stepping back out of the batter's box on every pitch whether it was close to them or not. Honestly, a good way of breaking a youngster from being afraid of being hit by a pitch is to have him stand in the batter's box and deliberately throw tennis balls at him so he can learn how to get out of the way without moving out of the box. But anyway, on this occasion this player was following his coach's orders to stay in the box. The only problem was this was a time when he was supposed to step out of the box. (The game of baseball is so confusing.) Unfortunately no one noticed all of these factors except for the umpire … me.

I stood behind the catcher with my right hand extended above my head, palm out toward the pitcher to indicate that the ball was not in play. The foul ball essentially had called time and I hadn't announced "Play ball" yet. In football the officials will wave their arms over their heads in a criss-cross motion to indicate a time out. To re-start the game, they rotate their arm in a clockwise fashion to signify to the timekeeper to start the clock. They can do this without any words because it is expected that the eyes of the players, coaches and spectators are watching the officials. That and they have the very loud whistles they blow constantly during the game. In baseball, though, it is all done by the voice and simple hand signals. There are no whistles, buzzers, or green flags to wave in this sport.

If the spectators are yelling and the players are yelling and the parents are shouting encouragement to their off spring, then no one is watching or listening to the umpire. Maybe I need to bring an air horn to the field to get their attention. But, instead, I do it with a very loud voice. Scorekeepers have asked me before the game starts if I would make my calls loud enough for them to hear from the bench. I attempt to reassure them that I am loud enough so that even the center fielder can hear the calls. From the first "Play ball!" call to the final out, I keep my voice loud and clear on all calls.

Pitchers, however, are in the zone and want to get on with their jobs. This young man had the ball back from his catcher. The catcher was in his position behind the plate. So the pitcher stepped on the rubber, wound his arms up and…. At the top of my lungs, I shouted, "Time out!"

The catcher nearly jumped out of his chest protector, but I accomplished the purpose; the pitcher stopped. As an umpire you must be in control of the game and be able to stop an errant, potentially dangerous action with only your voice.

I also related to the batter loud enough that the coach on third base could hear me, "When you are taking the signals from your coach, be sure to step out of the batter's box. That lets me and everyone else know you need time. Okay?"

He nodded his head. "And then, when you've got the signal, step back into the box and let me know you're ready to go.

"Okay? Let's go."

*   *   *

There are many things to keep in mind when playing an official game of baseball. The first is that anyone can ask for a time out at any time of the game but only the umpire can actually call a time out. And secondly, a time out cannot be called while a play is still taking place. (There are exceptions to that but I don't want to confuse the issue at hand. We'll get into those later. Okay?)

A few years ago when I was still doing the older boys' games (high school level and such), I had an experience that could be chalked up to the expression 'he should have known better.' With one out and a runner on second base, the batter lifted a fly ball to about the middle of left field. The runner was not sure if the ball would be caught and, although he would not be forced to advance if the ball did fall safely, he wanted to be ready to take third base should the opportunity present itself. Staying on second base to see if he could advance after the catch, he positioned himself to at least draw a throw.

As the only umpire working this game (my umpiring partner was a no show), I came out from behind the plate to position myself in foul territory between home and third to watch for catch/no catch, tag up if needed, and any play that might result at any base. In the meantime, the batter/runner advanced to first base and took a couple of steps toward second before the defensive player lost the ball in the sunlight or maybe he took his eyes off the ball to look at the runners and where he should throw once he caught the ball (always bring the ball in to second base, right players?).

When the ball fell to the ground, the runner on second took off for third base. The fielder quickly recovered the baseball and threw it in to third base making for a close play, close enough to cause the runner to slide to the bag. He was safe and I called him such.

But then the base runner did a foolish thing. While the batter/runner was still between first and second base, not sure where he wanted to go, the runner now on third indicated to me he wanted a time out to brush the dust off himself. Without waiting for my response (which would have been no), he stood up from the base and took a couple of steps away from the bag. The alert third baseman saw I had not awarded time and stepped out to where the runner stood to apply a tag,

"He's out!" I loudly declared with a high right arm extension to emphasize the call.

"No, no, no," the runner countered. "I called 'time.' I'm not out."

As the third baseman turned his attention to the batter/runner who was now trying to take second base, as I too directed my focus to the potential play there, I offered over my shoulder at the runner, who still stood there off the bag with outstretched arms asking "why?" "You can ask for 'time' anytime you want, son. You don't have it till I grant it. And, so far, I haven't granted it."

It was a lesson I hope he and his teammates learned very well that day. I didn't do it to be mean but because the batter/runner was still trying to advance, I couldn't stop the play by calling time for the benefit of the runner on third base. Where would I put the batter/runner? Back to first because he hadn't actually advanced to second? Then the offensive team would have been upset, arguing that I couldn't stop a play in progress. Place him on second base even though he hadn't actually gotten there yet? Oh, I would have heard it from the defensive squad then because he hadn't yet safely advanced to that bag. No, the play had to continue to its natural conclusion, so time could not be called.

One other thing that may have led to this play developing as it did was, even though this was fourteen-and fifteen-year-old youngsters playing this game, a player was acting as coach on third base and did not tell the runner to hold on the bag until time was given. It may be fun and in some cases necessary to put one of the players in the coach's box, but he must be aware of the game around him in order to coach the runners in more than just whether to slide or not. A coach, whether player or adult, needs to inform the runners of other developments of the game and be ever alert himself.

* * *

Another problem with the foul ball being tossed back directly to the pitcher is the umpire doesn't get the opportunity to check its condition. Now these younger pitchers are aged eight to twelve and most couldn't use a scuffed ball to aid a curve-ball pitch if I held a week-long seminar for them. Also I've had pitchers come to the set position and then take their empty hand out of the glove to rub their nose or wipe some perspiration off their forehead before going right back into the glove and the ball.

I will immediately call time before the pitcher proceeds with his delivery and start to walk out toward the mound. Toward the defensive team's dugout, I will look for the manager and invite him to join me before I get to the pitcher. More than one manager looked at me in disbelief of what I am indicating but it's my intention to stop the practice before it gets to be a habit with the pitcher and in the upper levels such action could not only have a balk called against him but also get him and his manager tossed from a game.

With all the mousse and gel and stuff kids use in their hair, it's a good source of a foreign element to add to the ball and aid in throwing a spitball or such. The pitchers are, of course, permitted to rub the ball between their bare hands or against their uniform to work out moisture or dirt but that must be done off the pitching rubber and preferably off the mound area.

Seriously I doubt if the younger players could throw a spitball, but I have seen some nasty knuckle-balls come in towards the batter only to veer off over the plate for a strike while the batter is sitting on his rump after falling away from the pitch. Even at the ten-year-old level these pitchers have been schooled on the art of throwing a knuckle-ball or otherwise making the ball dance as it comes toward the batter.

They may say it was only a curve ball, but this umpire wasn't hatched yesterday. I know a knuckler when I see one. And I have seen more than a few.

Generally all I would caution the pitcher about is that if he needs to go to his face or his mouth to wipe off some perspiration or something, he must wipe his hand off onto his uniform before going back into the glove. The rulebook indicates he is not allowed to wet his fingers even if he then wipes before going to the glove as long as he is within the pitching mound area. But, at this age level, I'll settle for their wiping off the hand first.

And as far as something on or askew with the foul ball going directly back to the pitcher, there have been times when another ball was tossed to the pitcher and the game ball that was fouled off never returning to the field. These balls I try to keep out of the game for numerous reasons.

The most obvious is that it might not actually be an official ball for this league. The teams in the Cal Ripken league use a different weight ball than in AAU and different manufacturers construct the balls with different materials. Such is why there are different official baseballs for each league and no two leagues use the same company and style of baseballs. They may even change their chosen firm from one season to the next. Also, if the baseball is one that had been used by the team previously, I have no idea how long that ball may have been used for infield practice, batting practice or even a previous game. After so much time of being hit, a ball can become lopsided or even out of round and therefore, when thrown or pitched, can turn unexpectedly in mid–air. If it had wound up in a water puddle but was allowed to dry off, it might be somewhat heavier than before and therefore drop quicker when pitched. Because of this for several years I've carried extra baseballs with me that I can contribute to the game. I attempt to rotate these balls after three or four games with newer (or even new) balls so they don't suffer the same fate of abuse.

When these players get to the thirteen-year-old level and beyond, the ball will dance as it comes into the batter. A fastball can really pop into the catcher's mitt and a change-up can rotate so slowly so as to almost let you count the stitches on the cover. In these games, it is not unusual for me to interject two brand new baseballs myself in order to prevent one from becoming too soft from frequent hits or even just popping into the gloves. And with a little mud or dirt on the ball or even stuck into a stitch, the ball becomes off-centered. Pitches with these types of balls I refer to as twist and shout: the ball twists around when pitched and the batter shouts as he swings and misses.

When I am called upon to umpire an upper level game, I pay strict attention to the pitcher's appearance and that of his glove. There are specific rules governing the design and manufacture of the gloves used by pitchers. They are lengthy but I feel noteworthy to the managers who should enforce them first, to the parents who can spend over a hundred dollars for a good leather glove only to have it be illegal for play, and especially to umpires who must know what is legal without having to open the rulebook on the field.

I have never taken a tape measure to a glove to check if its size adheres to the rules. The only objection I've ever heard from a manager concerning the opposing pitcher's glove is that it may have two shades of leather, which is a technical violation. Unless it's white or gray or the player has another glove to use for the game, I have let it slide, especially with the price of leather gloves for parents. The other exception is that I will not permit a pitcher to use a first baseman's mitt on the mound. The webbing of these gloves is the largest permitted in play to assist the first baseman to stretch just a couple of inches further to get that wide throw to the bag. But the pitcher does not need such advantage.

Pitchers will do what pitchers have always done—what *players* have always done—and umpires will draw the line when it needs to be enforced. But I do look out for the safety of the batters with doctored balls.

The Batter

It all starts with the batter. Pitchers may think the game revolves around them but if they didn't have the batter to throw the ball toward and past, there would be no point in having a pitcher.

There was a time during our umpiring that Buck took a couple of summers to also coach the first two seasons of a women's slow-pitch softball league in our hometown of Alliance, Ohio. I remember him coming home from that first practice with several stories he had to share. Most distinctly I remember him telling us that when the practice started he handed out index cards to each of the girls, telling them to write down their names, addresses, phone numbers, previous experience, and what position they wanted to play. Now this was a wide cross of women from their young twenties to one player who was in her fifties but had played fast-pitch softball for many years in other communities. There were maybe thirty girls (and I mean no disrespect by that term) present for that first practice. That number got whittled down real quick, though.

Once they had finished filling out the cards, Buck collected them and told the players to go play catch while he worked up a line-up for some practice. As he reviewed the index cards, he told us it was all he could do not to break out in laughter. At least six of the girls had indicated they had no experience playing baseball or softball before and their chosen position was batter.

That first season was fun as we discovered there were other teams with similar inexperienced players. There will be another tale of the Sugar 'n' Spice Sweeties in the next chapter.

*　　*　　*

One of the most asked questions of the umpire during the course of a game is "What's the count?" Each batter gets up to four pitches that are balls and up to three pitches that are strikes … except if he should hit the pitch into foul territory on the third strike and it is not caught. Then that strike does not count against him and he continues his turn at bat. Why are there four balls but only three strikes? I have no clue and neither does various Internet reference sites. If the batter should hit any pitch into foul territory before the third strike, that pitch does counts as a strike against him. Why? Again, I have no idea.

With this confusion afoot in the game, it's no wonder why the coaches and players are repeatedly asking, "What's the count?" This is why the home plate umpire (and no other umpire) has an indicator to keep track of the count. Obviously there are times when we either fail to record a pitch because of other things that are going on (passed ball, pick-off play, or runner trying to steal, just to name a few—thank goodness I have never had a streaker at one of my baseball games!) or flip the indicator twice for one pitch. When I have given the count using hand signals as well as verbal announcements, I have indicated two balls or two strikes by displaying my index and little finger in order to stretch it out as far as possible so as to avoid visual confusion.

Three balls are indicated by extending the index, little and middle fingers of the left hand. Strikes are always shown on the right hand. Recently I had been recruited to umpire at the high school level in Florida and was told that two balls or two strikes must be demonstrated by the index and middle fingers of the appropriate hand. To spread out the count on one hand is the sign for the Texas Longhorns, I was told, and we are playing baseball, not cheering for a college football team. Personally I try to be as cooperative as possible but have now found myself using both indicators throughout the game, although not at the same time … at least not yet.

With a 2-2 count on the batter in a twelve-year-old and under game, he proceeded to foul off the next three pitches, leaving the count at the same two and two. The eighth pitch was in the dirt and got past the catcher. As the defensive player jogged back to the backstop to retrieve the ball, the batter started to trot down to first base as if he had just received a walk. "Three balls and two strikes," I physically and verbally indicated to no one in particular. And that was just about who was paying attention.

The batter made it down to first base and the coach began talking strategy with him as the next batter stepped up to the batter's box. Again I said, this time maybe a little louder, "I've got three balls and two strikes," and then pointed down to first base, "on that batter there." It still didn't sink in as the next batter began to set himself into the batter's box and the pitcher, having received the ball back from the catcher, stepped onto the rubber.

Finally I had to call time in order to get anyone to understand what I was saying. "Batter, step out of the box," I began. "You're not up yet." I pointed again down to first base where the coach and the batter were finally watching me and in a loud voice stated, "That batter has a three ball and two strike count. He is not on first base."

Honestly, the coach then said, "Well, why didn't you say something?"

"Say something?" I repeated. "Coach, that's all I've been saying since the ball got away from the catcher." Whether or not he agreed with me, he sent the batter back to home plate and the next batter went back to his dugout. And, of course, wouldn't you know it, the next pitch was outside for ball four so the batter went down to first base anyway. But he had to wait until he had four pitches for balls recorded against him.

We were just lucky there had been no other runners on base at the time because technically if they had advanced because the batter went to first base, they would not have had to return to their previous bases because they actually would have stolen that base without a play being made against them.

Life Behind The Mask

Then there was the catcher who was aware of the count and alert enough that when the batter advanced to first with only three balls against him and, with the bases loaded, the runner on third walked down the line to cross home plate. The catcher had held on to the ball and took two steps up the third base line to meet the walking runner to tag him before he reached the plate. "This runner is out," I declared.

"No, no, no," the third base coach began as he came down the line. Please keep in mind time had never been called or even asked for and I continued to watch the other runners as this coach's actions were not really interfering with what else was going on in the field. "That was ball four and the batter gets first base," he presented. "All the runners have to advance one base so he," indicating the runner I had just called out, "gets home."

"Coach," I said without looking at him but now watching the runner who had been on second and had stopped between the bases and was actually talking with the defensive shortstop, "the count was only three balls on your batter. He needs to return here to complete his at-bat. So this runner was not forced to advance and he is out."

"Ah, come on," the coach disagreed, "you can't let something like that happen. You have to tell the batter he only has three balls on him before he goes to first base."

"And you need to make sure your runners know what the count is before they wander off the bases and get tagged out." I countered. Perhaps he didn't appreciate my sarcasm especially when I concluded my words by pointing out to the runner engaged in conversation off the base.

"Vincent," the coach yelled, "get back on base! There's only three balls on Davey!" With this, the catcher, still holding the ball, wound up to throw the spheroid to the shortstop but then thought better of it, realizing that if his shortstop didn't catch the ball, it could head off into left field and the runner might score anyway as the batter was returning to home plate. The runner safely returned to second base and the game continued, now with one out against the team at bat.

This is a very funny game.

*   *   *

Once the pitcher delivers the ball, the batter has three options of what to do. He may swing at the pitch, using any style of swing he wishes; he may not swing at the pitch; or he may move to get out of the way of the pitch. Of course there is also the option of any combination of the three, such as swinging while trying not to swing while trying to get out of the way of the pitch.

If he swings at the pitch, one of three things will happen: he will hit the ball into fair territory in which case he should drop the bat and run to first base; he will hit the ball into foul territory in which case he should drop the bat and run to first base only to be called back by the umpire (because the ball may actually be fair and, of course the batter isn't watching the ball so he really doesn't know where it was hit, right?); or he will miss the ball and will be charged with a strike. His swing can be a bunt, a half swing, or a full swing. He actually could just put the bat straight out over home plate and hope the ball hits it, and I have had the younger players do just that.

I want to offer here that being an umpire puts a person in a position where he can actually alter the English language and no one will object. I mean, where else can you take a one-syllable word like strike and make it a two-syllable declaration? Listen to the umpire when he calls "ste-rike."

It's two syllables. And then there is the call for a ball. If the umpire calls it at all (and I do), it's a quick short little "ball." Sometimes the l's aren't even audible.

Let's return to the batter swinging at the pitch. He swings and hits the ball. Whether it is fair or foul, they are told to run toward first base. Don't look at the ball. Don't look at the first baseman to see if he's getting ready for the throw because he may just be suckering you into thinking the throw is coming to him. Just run to first base with your feet moving and your ears open. You want to hear if the coach is sending you to second or telling you to run through the bag and stay at first. You also want to hear if the umpire is calling the ball foul. However, most of these batters are just like I am when golfing. I cheat a look at where the ball is going and therefore lift my head and bring my upper body with it. So the ball shanks off to the right.

When the batter is watching the ball, he is not sure where first base or the first baseman are and could very likely run into one or the other or both. It's happened and sometimes with painful results.

A hot grounder was headed toward the shortstop as the batter was headed for first base. His head was turned to the left as he watched the ball with his eyes while his feet got him closer to first base. This batter/runner was maybe nine years old and all of four feet tall and lucky if he weighed ninety pounds. On the other hand, the first baseman was at least ten years old and probably a head taller and at least 50 pounds heavier.

When the shortstop picked up the ball, he threw it directly to the first baseman. Now, as I said this first baseman was maybe four feet, six inches tall and many players looked up to him. But the throw from the shortstop was over the head of the six-foot-tall coach beside the base. The first baseman jumped up to at least get a glove on the ball right at the same time as the batter/runner bowled into him about waist high.

The batter/runner came to an instant stop as if he had run into a brick wall. But the fielder was pushed about three feet into foul territory by the impact. This was a field that was enclosed by fencing so the ball stayed in play but took an angle off the fence toward right field.

The first base coach did everything he could to get the batter/runner up and run to second base. I was very impressed that he did not physically pick the player up and push him toward the next base because I had seen that happen before. This young boy, though, was not going to make it to second base. He did manage to stand up on wobbly legs and take maybe three steps toward second before he fell down again. The right fielder had recovered the ball and threw it to second base so I called time to allow the coach to check his player for injuries.

I started to walk down toward first to see how the boy was feeling when I heard him ask, "Was I safe, Coach?"

"Yes, sir, son. You got your first hit." He pounded him on the back in congratulations and pulled him back toward the coach's box to brush him off.

He was beaming from ear to ear when I got to him. "Your first hit, eh?" I asked him to see if he had recovered his breath yet.

"Yep," he declared. Then he looked at me and asked, "Can I have the ball?"

I chuckled and looked at the coach. He didn't know what to say because he knew we would need that ball again during the game. I looked up at the first baseman to make sure he was all right, knowing full well he would never admit that this little kid could have hurt him. I then looked at the pitcher and told him to throw the ball to the first baseman. I wanted to see how this boy could move after landing on his side like he did. As expected the throw was not exactly where it was supposed to be and the player had to reach down to field it. But he showed no sign of injuries.

I held out my hand to accept the ball from the player. I then reached into the ball bag I had on my right hip and extracted the other game ball to give to the first baseman. "Thanks," I told him and watched him throw that ball to the pitcher. He was fine.

"Tell you what," I spoke to the batter/runner, "I'll put this one in my equipment bag and you come see me after the game. Okay?"

He agreed and couldn't stop beaming. I walked back

behind the backstop where I kept my equipment bag for my umpire's gear and a few extra used game balls that I collected during the year. I traded off this boy's souvenir for one in the bag and put it in for the new game ball. It also gave the first baseman a few extra moments to catch his breath and toss the ball back and forth with the pitcher. If asked, I'm sure he would contend he wanted to keep his pitcher warmed up while I was delaying the game with my actions. Whatever.

After the game, true to my word, the youngster came over and got his game ball from his first hit. I'm just a softie for the younger kids.

*　　*　　*

Most of the fields in Alliance had eight-row-tall wooden bleachers on either side set up by the City Park and Recreation Department, generally behind or beyond the benches for the players. These bleachers were usually filled with the parents and siblings not involved in the game. But sometimes they got involved whether they wanted to or not.

In the late 1970s, Earley's Hill Field #3 had the first base bleachers starting about ten feet past and behind the bench. These fields didn't have dugouts for the players, merely a twenty-foot-long bench. Neither were there tops on the backstops so foul balls would go out of the field of play rather easily. On this particular night, the bleachers were moderately filled with parents and the "G" League contest was a very good one. In the top of the fourth inning with a 1 and 1 count on the batter, one out and a runner on second, the batter fouled off the next pitch, a pop-up out of play towards the first-base bleachers. Instead of calling "Foul," for some reason I shouted "Incoming" to let the spectators know it was heading their way. From about the fifth row of bleacher seats, a middle-aged father suddenly leaped off the bleachers and flattened himself onto the ground as much as possible, covering his head with his arms. This man had been in 'Nam and I had just used the one word that meant so much to his very survival when he was in country.

Understand, I never served in the military but many friends had and the stories they've told made me glad I hadn't and sorry that they had. At that moment, when I saw him covering his head, the game became irrelevant. I had already called the ball as dead so I didn't need to do anything else at the field. Still with the outside balloon chest protector firmly in my left hand, I rushed over to this man just as he was getting up off the ground. Several people in the bleachers had no idea why he had just done what he did. I knelt down beside him to help him to his feet. "In country?" I asked and he nodded. "I'm sorry, man." I offered. "Just reflex on my part. I just said the word."

"And I reacted just like they taught us," he said. I could see a bit of a tear begin to form in his eye.

"But somebody didn't make it one day. Right?" I asked him as someone brought the foul ball back to me to put back into play. Again he nodded his head, unable to speak either from being too choked or out of embarrassment over what he had just done. My next action I have repeated to many a veteran before and since that day either in part or in whole. I gave the veteran a hug of appreciation. I told this man who had risked his life for my freedom, "Thank you for doing what you did." He was speechless. The normal reception that Vietnam veterans received upon their return home was far from friendly.

Putting the foul ball in my ball bag, I then shook this man's hand. He headed back to the bleachers and his family and I headed back to the field ever grateful for the freedoms that I have thanks to this man's service and that of his comrades.

*   *   *

Returning to the batter swinging at the pitch, one of the options he has is to bunt at the ball. The bunt is an interesting play, especially in youth baseball where it is not practiced enough to be used real well. A bunt is most often intended to catch the defensive team off guard and to advance a runner on first base by means of a sacrifice. If the batter successfully bunts the ball, it's down the third base line and either the third baseman charging up the line or the pitcher coming off the mound will get the ball and throw him out at first base while the other runner advances safely to second or more if the shortstop doesn't rotate around to cover third. If the catcher is the player to field the bunt, the batter has a chance of being safe on first because once he picks up the ball, the catcher in full equipment has to take one or two more steps away from home plate in order to throw to the first baseman without hitting the batter/runner.

Why does he not want to hit the batter/runner? Probably because he doesn't want to hurt him. That is the only reason I as an umpire can see. The batter/runner is required to run on the foul side of the base line. The catcher will pick up the ball in fair territory and throw it to the player covering first base in fair territory. If his throw hits the batter/runner as he is traveling to first base and he is on or inside the fair line then the batter/runner is guilty of interference. If interference is called, the batter/runner is out, the ball is dead and all runners must go back to the base they occupied before the pitch was thrown.

The batter/runner is required to run within a three-foot wide lane on the foul side of the base path during the last half of the distance to first base in order to avoid being in the path of a thrown ball or a fielder attempt to recover the batted ball or catch a thrown ball.

So if the catcher's throw were to hit the batter/runner and he is not in that lane, it is considered to be interference. Remember, though, the key words in that rule are "in the umpire's judgment" if there was interference. Most umpires will see it as interference but not deliberate because the batter/runner couldn't have seen the throw coming from behind him. The rule, however, doesn't distinguish whether the batter/runner's actions were deliberate or not. It's just as a batter being hit by a pitch. If the pitcher didn't mean to do it, it doesn't count? No, if the batter is hit by a pitch, the ball is dead and the batter is awarded first base within the parameters of the rule. If the batter/runner is hit by a thrown ball while running to first base and he is outside that three-foot lane (and most are), then it is interference. The batter/runner is out and all other runners return to their prior bases so the value of the sacrifice is eliminated.

Let me also add that first base is in fair territory and that is where that batter/runner is heading so at that point he must be in fair territory, but the rulebook states he may not be on the fair side of the base line during that last half of the distance. Well, what do you know? Another point of conflict within the rules. There's got to be at least an implied exception in there someplace.

*　*　*

The catcher's chatter is part of the game. In the older divisions, the players on different teams may actually go to the same school and therefore have some classes or friends in common or even be friends themselves.

There have, in fact, been times when I have felt to be the odd man out of a conversation at home plate. I have also heard, because I do not even try to get involved in a conversation so as neither team could argue I was distracting one or the other player, the catcher and batter going over homework assignments for a shared class. As long as each can still concentrate on their tasks at hand, I have no problem with that (as long as the catcher stops the baseball before it hits me, that is.)

There was one instance, though, where I did have to jump in concerning a catcher's chatter. Both players were high school aged and the teams apparently played each other before as the catcher was engaged in some trash talk with this batter. With no runners on base and one out already recorded in the half-inning, the catcher was laying it on thick, telling the batter he had just called for an inside curve ball because he knew the batter couldn't hit that pitch. The ball was too far inside for ball one. His chatter for the next pitch implied it would be another inside pitch to tie up the batter. However, the pitch was actually across the outside corner for strike one. "Oh, can't hit those outside balls, eh?" the catcher taunted. But again crossing up his friend, the batter, the third pitch was inside. I have seen batters try to sneak a peek back at the catcher before the pitch is thrown, trying to see where he is set up to get a jump on the ball. But the catchers are aware of this and change their position two or three times before each pitch. I know because I learned years ago to just stay put behind home plate and not try to hide behind the catcher who is trying to be a moving target. That would be just when a ball that zigged when I tried to zag would plunk me on an arm or other body part. In this case, though, the batter had guessed outside pitch and had already committed to swinging at that outside pitch. Granted he did his best to pull his upper body out of the inside pitch's path while unable to stop his swing. One ball, two strikes.

The catcher chuckled and then told the batter the next pitch would be a fastball down the middle. I was thinking it would probably be just the opposite, being a change-up low on the knees. And I was kind of right but the batter had guessed such also and never offered at the slowball pitch that actually skipped across the plate after hitting the ground in front for ball two.

The batter, who hadn't said a thing at all, now offered, "You want to try that fastball again?"

"Sure," replied the catcher, "if you want to strike out." The catcher kept up his chatter as the pitcher delivered the ball. But, within that chatter, he unintentionally crossed the line and I heard the instruction "swing." Outside of profanity, that is probably the only word of the English language not to be said around a batter. Unfortunately the batter did swing at the pitch and missed for what would have been strike three. That call, though, I never made. Instead I loudly called "Time!" and stepped out in front of home plate with my back to the pitcher, facing the catcher. He had a confused look on his face but I immediately took steps to clarify the situation for him.

"We have no pitch here," I announced to both benches. "The catcher used the word 'swing' to the batter. That," I continued now focusing directly on the catcher who had half-stood up but still had the ball in his mitt, "is not permitted." I lowered my voice so only he and the batter could hear me as I said, "You know better than that. I've heard you talk with every batter up here. I have no problem with your chatter. In fact, I love it. But you know better, son."

Sheepishly he offered, "Yes, sir. It just kind of slipped out. Won't happen again, sir."

I dropped my hard-butt attitude. "Okay. It's done. It's forgotten."

Directing myself to the batter who was still standing in the batter's box despite having just swung at strike three, I said, "You've got two balls and two strikes," with the accompanying hand signs for all to see. "Now, let's go."

I heard no objections from either bench to my unorthodox solution (the rulebook would advise me to have called strike three, retire the batter and warn the catcher and his manager but remember these players, even at this age level, are still learning the game and this was an important lesson for everyone so I let this one slide with no unnecessary punishments).

I stepped back behind home plate. The catcher offered his apologies to the batter and, unfortunately, lost his chatter for a while.

Compared to the seemingly constant noise of before, the

quiet around home plate now seemed deafening. I felt guilty breaking it with my pitch calls, but it had to be done.

Two pitches later and the batter was finally retired on a swinging strike. The catcher again found his voice the next inning, though guarded with what he was saying. It was a lesson learned that evening.

*   *   *

In the bunt scenario, the two biggest flaws I have seen in having eight-to twelve-year-old try to bunt is they don't know how to hold the bat and too many young players have what I have called happy feet.

When a batter holds the bat for a full swing, he has both hands wrapped around in a tight grip near the knob of the bat. When they slide their back hand (right hand for right handed batters, left hand for left handed batters) for that bunt, they sometimes forget to cradle the bat between the thumb and index finger. As a result they still have their fingers around the bat and therefore in front of the bat and potentially in the way of the incoming pitch.

With no count on the batter, no outs and a runner on first, the ten-year-old batter received the bunt sign from his third base coach. I knew it was coming and so did basically everyone else on the field. The third and first basemen were drawn in toward the plate and the second baseman cheated toward first to cover the bag. The shortstop stood two steps away from second base for the throw should it come there. This field arrangement left a wide open lane for a high bouncer down the lines and practically gave third base to the runner should he want to take it because the left fielder wasn't moving in yet to cover that bag.

The batter squared around to bunt as the pitcher delivered the ball. It was coming in tight and the batter extended his bat to strike the ball. When the ball hit the bat, it sounded very odd and dropped right in front of home plate in fair territory. The batter, however, made no attempt to run to first. Instead he stood in the batter's box with the bat still in his left hand, shaking his right hand to shake off the sting of it being hit by the pitch.

"Strike one!" I shouted. "Ball is dead!"

"What?" screamed the offensive team manager. "He hit the ball. It's a fair ball." By the time he finished his sentence he was directly in front of me. This was not the first time in this game that he had come out before asking for time to argue a call with me and I was very close to running him out. But I really didn't want to do that in front of the players. So I had been putting up with a little more than I should have. I turned to the batter who was still trying to shake the sting off.

"Did that ball hit you, son?" I asked.

"Yeah, it hit my hand," he answered. Then he suddenly realized. "Do I get first base?"

"No," I replied. "Did you swing at the ball?"

"No," was his response. "I bunted it."

At this point I turned back to the manager. "If a batter is hit by a pitch that is in the strike zone or that he is trying to hit, the ball is dead and the pitch is a strike."

"What kind of a dumb rule is that, Blue?" the manager queried.

"Ah, one that is in the rulebook you supposedly read before the season started." I answered very sarcastically. "Now, unless you want to argue balls and strikes with me, I suggest you get back to the bench while you still can stay in the game."

"You show me where that's a rule," he now shouted. "You're just making it up. I'm going to protest."

I turned to face the spectators and bench of the defensive team and announced, "The manager wants to place this game under protest. I need the home team scorekeeper and opposing manager out here now, please."

They complied with my request and stood beside me as I returned my attention to the manager. At this point, my entire object was to show this manager he was wrong and would not see the end of the game tonight. I explained to the opposing team's manager (who was the home team) what my call had been and that it was in accordance with the rulebook. I then explained the offensive manager was protesting that there is no such rule.

"Tom," the home manager said to his counterpart. "It's in there. He's absolutely right." He asked his scorekeeper for the rulebook in her scorer's folder. She handed it to him and he went straight to one of the more than 16 instances of except or exception although this one is actually prefaced by unless.

While the home manager was reading the rule to his counterpart, I checked the batter to make sure he was okay and there were no broken fingers, something that his own manager hadn't even considered, so intent he was on arguing with me about the rules.

When the home manager finished his recitation, I asked both managers if they had any questions. None. The rule being read and shown to the offensive manager, I quietly informed him he was being ejected from the game for arguing a ball or strike call and must leave the park.

I did not try to make a big production of his ejection or show him up but I did demonstrate to him that I was right and he hadn't read the rulebook. I have absolutely no problem with a manager coming out to question a call or an application of a rule but when they haven't read the rulebook and accuse me of not knowing the rules, that upsets me more than I can afford to show on the field. The fact that I can remember these events years later demonstrates just how much they scar me.

* * *

The second major problem of youngsters bunting without proper instruction is they want to move their feet with their body when they turn to bunt the ball. They must not have either foot on the ground completely out of the batter's box when they make contact with the ball. If they do (this might be sounding like a broken record but this is the result), the batter is out, the ball is dead and no runners may advance.

So when the batter turns to face the pitcher in order to bunt, he must keep his back foot inside the batter's box, keeping in mind that the line is actually inside the box. The best way I have seen to accomplish this is to just pivot on the toes of the back foot to bring the body around. Also keep in mind the two specific conditions of that foot to result in the batter being called out just for hitting the ball: his foot must be entirely outside of the batter's box (the lines are inside the box), and the offending foot must be on the ground when contact is made. Unless the batter's foot is behind or on home plate, it is sometimes difficult for the umpire positioned behind the catcher to see if the foot is entirely out of the batter's box when the entire foot is not on the ground. Very seldom have I called a batter out for this on bunts, but I have warned the batter and his manager to be mindful of the location of the feet for bunts.

I have had teams so far ahead and, despite their best efforts, couldn't get a put out against them, courteously and deliberately had their batters step out of the batter's box while hitting the ball just to make that third out.

The scenario is with two outs, the defensive team pitcher either couldn't hit the strike zone and the batters are just walking around the bases (in these cases I have been known to go big on the strike zone after letting the manager know to have his players get the bats off their shoulders) or the batters are slamming the ball all over the field and the defensive (or defenseless) fielders can't make the proper plays to record the final out.

In the nine-and ten-year-old division, I had a team consistently score seven runs or more each inning and take a sizable double-digit lead into the third inning. After they had batted completely around their order and had no outs recorded against them, I indicated to the manager who was coaching at third base, that I was going even bigger with the strike zone. I had already extended it to beyond the black sides of home plate. He shook his head negatively and asked for time.

As we met halfway down the third base line, he asked me, "What do we have to do to get out?"

It was a humorous question and my first answer was, "Don't get to first base."

"That'll work." He chuckled. "Anything else?"

I thought for a moment before I suggested, "When your batters square to bunt, step on home plate. That's a sure out and a dead ball."

"Even better." He went to his on-deck batter to pass the word.

When this batter stepped in, he looked down at the coach for the sign and then said, "Oh, boy. A bunt." He tried to sound sinister with it but it wound up being comical.

With the infielders pulled in for the bunt, the first pitch came in. He turned and planted his right foot square on home plate as he reached for the pitch with his bat. The ball, however, was well over his head, well over the catcher's head and, thankfully, well over my head but still he reached for it so I called it: "Strike one."

As the catcher went back to recover the ball, the batter said to me, "But my foot was on home plate. Am I out?"

"No, you have to hit the ball when your foot is on the plate." I advised him. "A swing and a miss isn't good enough here. But you do have one strike."

With the ball back to the pitcher, the batter set himself up again for a bunt. This time he was successful and, with the ball in fair territory I loudly declared, "Dead ball! Batter is out! He was standing on home plate when he hit the ball! Dead ball!"

The youngster beamed as he went back to the bench. The next batter didn't try to step on home plate but did swing wildly at every pitch offered and was retired on three pitches, all well outside the strike zone.

For the final out the manager sent the runner from third as the pitch was coming into the plate. Halfway down the base path, he just stopped.

The catcher started down the line to start a run down but the runner didn't move until the catcher tagged him out.

On one hand it was sad to see it happen that way but also beneficial to see the effort that the one team put forth to be courteous. They could have continued to pile on the runs until the fifth inning but didn't.

*   *   *

If the batter decides not to swing at the pitch, the umpire has two choices. Was the pitch within the strike zone? If so he therefore calls it a strike. Or was it outside the zone and therefore is declared a ball? If it was far enough outside the strike zone, everybody agrees with the call and all is right with the world. But, if it is close, regardless of the call, half the people love the ump and the other half want to kill the blind man. I have sat in the stands in civilian clothes and heard one mother declare the home plate umpire must have gone to the Ray Charles School of Umpiring. (By the way, to the best of my knowledge, there is no such place.)

It is important to remember when judging a ball or strike call is that the strike zone is a three-dimensional object and, if *any part* of the ball enters *any part* of the strike zone, it is a strike. Keep in mind, a ball or strike call is a judgment call and cannot be argued. But it will be regardless. The umpire must be deaf to the objections of either side and not attempt to make up for a bad call (which we all make but *never* admit to).

Personally, I fell into the bad habit of occasionally adding a description to the location of a ball pitch such as outside, inside, high or just missed. It's a terrible hole to dig for yourself because when you don't elaborate on the pitch, the manager wants to know where it was and he

93

knows you will tell him because you have in the past. This just invites a comment to the pitcher to the effect of, "Guess you're gonna have to put it right down the middle." And the worse point of that comment is I have been known to remark under my breath (but those doggone catchers are always close enough to hear), "That would be where the strike zone is, sir."

When I moved to Florida a few years ago and umpired youth games here, I told myself, "Don't describe the pitch. Just call it." And, for the most part, I try to remember that. But still occasionally I'll add that extra word or two to a ball call. I have also literally bitten my tongue more than once to stop that descriptive adjective.

Another game I was watching I heard a rookie umpire not call a pitch a ball but rather only used the descriptive word of outside, away, too low and such. I made a point of speaking with him after the game and advising him not to get in the habit of such words but just call the pitch either a ball or a strike and move on to the next pitch. Honestly he wasn't even aware he was doing it but next time I saw him, it was ball and strike.

*   *   *

Now, if the pitch hits the batter (and I am amused by how the rulebook refers to it as "touches the batter"; makes it sound less violent, don't you agree?), he is entitled to first base. As we have already seen, such is not always the case. He must at least make an effort to get out of the way of the pitch. He must certainly not move in such a manner as to place himself into the path of the pitch. And he must not swing at the pitch while trying to get out of its way.

Another instance is he must be sure when he is getting out of the way of the pitch that he gets the bat out of the way as well. I can't tell you how many times at all age groups the batter ducks down from a pitch around his head but leave the bat hanging up in the same position as before. Hence when the ball comes in where his head was just a few seconds ago, it now hits the bat. The worst occasion of such is when the pitched ball hits the bat while the batter is crunched down out of the way and the ball goes fair. Nine times out of ten, this batter will be out at first base when a fielder, usually the pitcher, recovers the ball and throws to the bag while the batter is still crunched down in the batter's box.

When the ball hits the bat and goes into foul territory, it is a foul ball. As the batter stands back up with a disbelieving look on his face, I will often remind him that he needs to bring the bat down with him. "That ball obviously has a mind of its own," I would caution the player. "It was gonna hit something. And the poor bat was just hanging there." The humor helps the hurt a little and he'll remember next time ... I can only hope.

When the pitch is coming straight into the batter's chest, he can try to make himself small and get out of the way or he can fall on his butt to avoid getting hit.

Just the other night I had a lead-off batter in a twelve and under contest ready to hit the first pitch over the fence.

However, the pitcher had been throwing very much inside during his warm-ups so I was alert to anything (and anything can happen at any time). "Play ball!" I instructed and the pitcher went into his wind up.

The ball came in very tight and chest high. The batter pulled himself up small to get out of the way but the ball found its way to the knob of the bat and the batter's hand. Which it hit first was my only question.

As the ball fell harmlessly into the catcher's area behind home plate and he picked up the ball, I indicated "Time" and pulled the batter back towards me away from the catcher. "Your hand okay, son?" I asked him.

He had that shaking-thing going on to throw off the sting. "That was close, Blue," he told me.

"Where did it hit you?" I inquired. He indicated on the little finger of his left hand. "And it got the bat, too, didn't it?"

"I suppose," he said.

I turned and announced to the field, "Foul ball. Strike one."

I had just made half the crowd happy and half the crowd angry.

Both managers came out to question my call. I explained the pitch hit the bat and was therefore a foul ball. The batter interjected, "But it hit me."

"And the bat. Foul ball." I repeated. "Folks, it's far too early in this game to have this argument already. Okay?"

With considerable grumbling the managers agreed and returned to their benches. The batter grounded out to second with the next pitch and the game was on.

The other side of this situation can be when the ball soundly hits the hands and not the bat. When that point is clear, the batter is awarded first base, as long as the pitch was not in the strike zone or he was not swinging at it.

On one such occasion, the defensive manager in this ten-to twelve-year-old contest was up out of the dugout faster than I thought this overweight man could move. "It hit the bat," was his objection.

"No," I said calmly, "it hit his hand."

"But the bat was in the hand," he countered.

"Yep, sure was," I agreed. This was going to be a fun exchange I decided right then.

"And the hand is part of the bat."

It was all I could do to avoid laughing. "It's what?" I asked being totally unprepared for this argument.

"The hand is part of the bat," he repeated. And he was dead serious.

I turned to the batter standing there, not realizing it was the next batter up as the youngster who was touched by the pitched ball already ran down to first base. "Batter," I instructed, "drop the bat." He complied. "See, coach," I indicated, "the hands didn't go with the bat. They're still on the ends of his wrists; right where God put them." I was being a smart alec with my approach but this manager would not let the point drop.

He thought for a few seconds before continuing. "Well, that's the wrong batter," he finally said.

It was all I could do not to break down right there. "We could get a hundred players out here and in every case the hands are part of the player, not the bat. The runner gets first base." I then took a step to the manager and placed my hand on his right shoulder as I pointed down to the end of the third base dugout, "And you get to go back there and have a seat, please, sir."

The hands are part of the bat. I'm still shaking my head in disbelief on that one.

*   *   *

It's the little things in life that sometimes account for the most important results.

In an upper division game, I believe fourteen-and fifteen-year-old players, the game had been progressing smoothly, which is usually when something blows up in your face. Probably the bottom of the third inning and the first batter of the half-inning came up to take his place in the right-handed batter's box. But something was strangely different about this player. I couldn't immediately put my finger on it but just to be on the safe side, I hesitated in getting behind the catcher. Then it dawned on me. This batter had no helmet. I kept my hand extended in the timeout position for the pitcher and asked the batter, "You ready to go?"

"Yeah, sure. Go ahead," was his reply, thinking I was holding time for him to get set in the batter's box.

I waited until he turned to look at me and then nonchalantly tapped my left hand on top of my head. "Forget something, did you?" I inquired.

At first he didn't understand what I was telling him then he tapped his hand on top of his own head and didn't feel a batting helmet.

"Hey, David," he called to the batter on deck, "throw me out a helmet."

Without missing a beat, I extended my hand toward David as if to tell him to hold up on that helmet. The batter looked at me like I had lost my mind. First I point out that he absent-mindedly forgot his helmet, now I'm telling the on-deck batter not to throw one out to him.

Quietly, I suggested to the batter, "Please?"

He gave me one of those looks I had probably given my own mother when she would do something like this to me. 'Like, are you for real?'

I continued to hold my hand out to David and followed it with a look as if to say, 'not yet.' Finally the batter acknowledged my request: "Dave, *please* throw me out a helmet."

It wasn't exactly what I was looking for but I lowered my hand and nodded to David who then tossed a helmet to the batter. From behind the backstop I heard two mothers applaud my efforts. One said to the other, "I like this guy. He makes them say 'please.'"

I turned in their general direction, because I really couldn't tell who exactly had spoken, I commented, "Momma taught me manners and I'm not too old not to use them still."

One of the mothers gave me a thumbs up sign and I felt better for trying to get that lesson across to another generation. We are only as good as we teach the next generation to be.

*   *   *

Everyone has a trophy. Even if it's just a cheap little "World's Greatest Dad" trophy, everyone has something. And, in the game of baseball, there are many opportunities to win trophies: MVP of a tournament, Golden Glove, Rookie of the Year or Cy Young Award just to name a few. But sometimes it's the things that are never intended to be trophies that carry the most meaning.

I spoke of the young man who got his first hit (and knocked over the bigger first baseman at the same time) wanting to have the baseball as a souvenir, as his trophy. I know of chapters who make a big deal out of awarding trophies at the end of the season to various players and of course there is the time-honored tradition of selecting a player for the game ball. As an umpire I am not supposed to play favorites and I don't think this is doing such. I've mentioned how few baseballs are available for each game and frequently a ball must be removed if it has gotten overly scuffed or wet. I also pointed out that I carry extra baseballs myself to substitute into the game just in such cases. Well, there are always other reasons for removing a baseball from the game.

In Manatee County, I had a game at the G. T. Bray fields in the twelve-year-old and under division. It was early in the spring season and admittedly one of the teams wasn't as strong as its opponent. But that didn't stop the players from giving it their best and working for that victory.

In the bottom of the third inning, they were behind by maybe three runs. You couldn't tell it from their level of enthusiasm, though. With one out already recorded and a runner on first base, the batter quickly had a one ball and one strike count on him before fouling off five pitches in a row. Some were close but could have been called a ball if he had let them go. Finally he tagged one high to right field. I felt certain the right fielder would get under it and I have to admit he moved back quickly and was set to make the catch except that 210 foot deep fence got in his way and the ball fell harmlessly on the ground on the other side of the fence as a home run.

The youngster circled the bases with the biggest smile on his face. Never mind the fact that he just brought his team to within a run of their opponent. No, his smile was for his first home run. And he was so proud of himself. As were his teammates who met him at home plate.

The inning progressed and his team scored no further runs during their turn at bat. While the teams changed positions on the field, I walked over to the home team bench to see if the baseball had been returned to the field. One of the coaches handed me a baseball I knew wasn't the one that had been hit over the fence. I said I needed that ball back.

"That was his first home run," explained the coach. "We like to give the boys the ball as an award."

"Coach," I objected, "you know we can't do that. We play with a limited number of baseballs and have to keep them in the game. Besides, what's he gonna do with a souvenir baseball during the game when he's on the field?"

"Oh, we'll hold it back here until after the game and then give it to him," he explained indicating where the ball was being kept.

I held my hand out and said, "Sorry, I need it here, please." The umpire was going to be mean here.

Reluctantly the coach gave me the baseball, which I put in my pants pocket behind the ball bag. "Now, which player is it that hit the homer?" I asked. He indicated the right fielder and I inquired, "Are his folks here tonight?" The coach said his mother was in the stands and pointed in the general area.

"Okay, when he comes back in this inning, I need to see him." I said and then returned to home plate for the next half-inning.

At the conclusion of the half-inning, I walked back over to the home team bench again and asked for the young man to come out to me, in front of the dugout. I make it a practice not to go into a dugout during the game unless it is absolutely necessary so as not to even allow a misconception of my actions.

He came out, although I'm sure he had no idea why. "Young man, was that you that hit that ball over the fence last inning?" I asked.

He wasn't sure why I was asking but acknowledged it was. "You know we can't have that." I said. "We need all of the baseballs to stay in the game." I reached into my pocket and pulled out his home run ball. "Now this one has gotten scuffed and we can't use it anymore." I handed it to him. "You think you may have someplace to put this one?"

He looked at me and then to his coach who understood what I was doing. Once again that big smile came over the young boy's face. "I'm sure I can, sir," he said. "Thanks."

"Now, go find your mother and have her hold it for the rest of the game," I told him. As he started to walk away back towards the dugout, I offered, "And congratulations. That should be the first of many."

"Yes, sir," he said with a wave as his mother met him at the entrance to the dugout, waving her thanks to me as well.

Of all the awards I have won in my life, I have to honestly say my most important personal trophy is from baseball. It is the old wooden bat (back in the days when we used actual wooden bats, not these aluminum ones of today) that I used to hit my first home run when I was nine years old at Earley's Hill field #3 over fifty years ago. It's been cracked and taped back together and really can't ever be used again. But I still have it and I know why. It's my own little trophy. Everyone should have at least one.

Runners and Wannabe Runners

There are times during the warm summers that working behind the plate can make for a very exhausting afternoon. The umpire is out on the field for the entire game. Unlike the players who get to go into the dugout or at least sit on the bench after each half-inning, get a drink of water and recoup from the heat, the umpire is out there for the complete game. I'm not complaining because, in some cases the catcher being able to take that break every half-inning could be a bad thing. On this particular occasion the catcher for this eleven-and twelve-year-old's contest had apparently gotten used to catching for ten minutes or so and then going to sit down for the next ten minutes or so. So when a long half-inning on the field presented itself, he was not ready for it. It was late June in Ohio but the day was exceptionally warm, in the mid–80s with humidity in the 90% range. Or so it seemed.

Seven batters and maybe one out made for a long spell in the sun for the bottom of the fourth inning. Add to this that the pitcher was getting tired as well and therefore not throwing as well as he had; the catcher had a few balls get by him. He'd have to get up, retrieve the ball, throw it back to the pitcher and then retake his position.

With runners on second and third and only one out, the batter had gone to a 3-1 count. The next pitch was outside for ball four. It glanced off the catcher's mitt and rolled to his right by two and a half feet or so. Not even thinking what he was doing, the catcher took off his mask with his right hand and pulled the loose ball back to him with the mask.

"Two bases," I shouted to everyone in general. I then pointed to the runner who was idly standing on third base. "You get home, son," I told him. Then I pointed to the runner who had just stepped off second base. "Third and home, runner. Two bases," were my instructions to him.

The defensive manager was bewildered as he came out

from his bench area. "What are you doing, Blue?" he asked while he was still less than halfway to the home plate area.

By this point the catcher has stood up and was holding the ball in the mitt. "Catcher," I spoke to him, "how did you pick up that ball?"

"With my glove," he indicated while showing the ball was still in the webbing.

"And how did it get there?" I asked of him while the manager was asking what that had to do with anything.

He looked at the ball in the glove and then over to his right hand that still held the mask. In just that fraction-of-a-second he realized what he had done and dropped the mask like it had suddenly become a thousand degrees hot. It almost hit his manager's foot about the same time the runner from second was touching home plate, though he still didn't know why.

"All runners are entitled to two bases, coach." I said. "I can't help it, but that's in the book."

"Where?" was all he could muster.

"It's got to be in the runner's section," I suggested. "What's that? Five hundreds? No, I think it's sevens. Check it out, won't you, please?"

He and I had met before on numerous occasions and he knew that I was very well versed in the rulebook. There were even occasions when I could tell the manager who was questioning my call of a rule as to what page number in the book he would find the specific regulation. He returned to his bench not exactly sure what had just happened. I saw him heading for his scorekeeper, the person on the bench who usually kept the rulebook during the game. Now I will acknowledge that according to the book the ball was not dead and the batter who was now entitled to second base could continue to advance but he would be at peril of being put out by the defensive team. However, since he was stopped on second base (although I'm sure he had no idea why he was there and not just first base) and showed no indication of advancing further, I held up my hand and verbally indicated "Time." I hadn't awarded it before when the manager came out because technically we were still in the middle of a play, except no one realized it but me.

Moving around to in front of the plate to brush it off, I gave the manager a minute or so to look up the appropriate rule. When I finished, I suggested to the catcher, "You might want to throw that back to the pitcher?" I indicated the ball still in his glove. "He may need it." I added with a chuckle. He complied and then went about picking up his mask while I stole a glance over to the manager who was looking into the rulebook. Slowly he raised his head to look at me and nodded in agreement.

He had found the rule and I was right.

In all seriousness I have to admit that a couple of days before this unusual play I was reading about a major league catcher (I believe it was Ray Fosse but don't quote me on that) who had done pretty much the same thing. It's not a very usual call but I was grateful that I knew the appropriate correction to apply.

Adjusting the mask back on my head, I instructed, "Batter up. Let's get back to work. Play ball!"

*   *   *

Among the reasons I prefer umpiring in the younger divisions is because they play the game with 100% all the time. They don't coast because they know they can still win giving say 80% or they still believe they can win every game. And just because someone may have told them the other team is considered better than them, they still try their best knowing some days the baseball takes strange bounces and the lesser team can win. But probably most importantly, they don't try to take shortcuts to win. They always do their best and are taught to always look their best.

Players must keep their shirttails tucked in. It's an

appearance thing, yes, but it is also a safety issue. I work in a business casual office during the day and believe me if I could have my shirttail out, I would do it in a heartbeat. But I can't.

Part of the safety issue for the players is so they don't get their equipment tangled up in a loose shirt. During practices I have seen players in the field with their long shirttails out only to get the gloved hand tangled up in it as the batted ball scoots by them to the outfield or, in the case of an outfielder, to the fence if the field has one for extra bases.

I have also seen players at the plate get the end of their bat twisted up in a loose shirt or shirttail because they leaned the bat against their abdomen to tighten up their batting gloves or such and then struggle to get the knob end free from the clothing material.

But the two most important reasons to tuck that shirttail in involve the batter and the pitcher. Every player should have his (or her) shirttail tucked in at all times but let's just focus on these two players for now. If the pitcher has a loose shirttail or an extremely loose fitting shirt, it can add to the difficulty of the batter being able to pick up the ball on delivery. It's the same as a pitcher having a multi-colored glove making it harder to find the ball. In making it harder to see the ball in order to hit it, it also becomes an issue of being able to see and avoid the ball if necessary. So pitchers, please, tuck in that shirttail. And parents, I've mentioned elsewhere at great length about being aware of the rules when purchasing an expensive leather glove for your sons or daughters. That multi-colored glove may look nice and might be able to stand out to be found a whole lot easier in the bottom of the closet, but it might also be illegal for a pitcher to use. And, let's be honest, every parent wants their child to be the star of the game and that means being the pitcher.

Of course there is the player who, as the batter, hits the

game winning home run. And the batter needs to be able to freely swing the bat so some degree of looseness with the shirt is permitted. I specifically remember one batter in an under–12 contest who had his shirt puckered loosely about his waist so it wasn't too tight to hamper his swing. With no runners on, the batter had a 0-2 count when the next pitch came in very tight. It was a good pitch and perfect placement, meant to back off the batter a little in order to set up the next pitch to be on the outside corner of the plate (although at this age level, I doubt if too many pitchers think that way—their managers may, but not the pitchers).

As the batter straightened up to get out of the way of the ball, his shirt moved in an unusual manner; such that I wasn't entirely convinced the ball didn't brush him. But I wasn't sure it had hit him. So, without making a call one way or the other and, while the catcher threw the ball back to the pitcher, I stepped forward and took the batter gently by the shoulder and lightly moved him and myself away from home plate.

"You okay?" I asked.

"Sure. Why not?" was the youthful honest response.

"The ball didn't get you, did it?" I inquired.

"Oh, no. I moved back away," he said.

I brushed at his loose shirt as if to get a bug off him. I didn't see any indication that the ball had brushed him so I then returned to my position behind home plate and indicated the count was 1 ball and 2 strikes. The coach from first base yelled down the line. "The ball hit him, didn't it? He gets first base. Right?"

"He says it didn't hit him, coach," I said adjusting my mask to get back to work.

I heard the coach say something like, "We've got to work on that 'honesty' thing."

Without taking my vision off the pitcher and the action about to take place in front of me, I offered loud enough for the coach and apparently most of the spectators to hear, "I like that 'honesty' thing right where it is, thank you very much."

I could hear several of the parents behind the backstop chuckle at my response and could see the coach at first just drop his head onto his chest and shake it from side to side indicating I wasn't supposed to hear his previous comment. This ump ain't blind and he sure isn't deaf, either.

*   *   *

Let's get a little more complicated now with multiple base runners. When you have two runners on the same base at the same time, the answer of who is legal and who is not is easy to apply. The trailing runner is out because the lead runner hasn't yet surrendered possession of the base.

Now what happens when there are three runners trying to possess the same base at the same time? Don't laugh for I have had it happen. This, too, is an easy answer because the same rule applies. The lead runner is still the only runner to have legal possession of the base. If both other runners are tagged while in contact with the base, they are both out. Except…

This truly happened in a nine-and ten-year-old contest. With runners on first and second and no one out (with the Infield Fly Rule in effect), the batter lifted a high fly ball to right field beyond an infield fly possible catch. With the third base coach screaming to the runner to stay on the bag, the runner on second followed the instructions. However, with the batter/runner barreling down on him at first, the runner on first base panicked and took off for second with the ball still in the air and the batter/runner hot on his heels. The ball fell harmlessly to the ground and the right fielder picked it up. Throwing to second base, as any good right fielder has been told to do, the second baseman received the ball and turned around to see all three runners standing on second base. "Tag 'em," shouted his coach while the offensive team coach was beseeching his players to run. My first thought was I was about to see a Chinese fire drill on the base or an episode of the Keystone Kops. The runners, though, had been told before that you cannot be called out if you are standing on the bag (one of those urban legends that are soooo wrong) so they all three held fast. That really didn't help them in this case.

The order of tagging the runners was important as to who was out and who was not. If the runner originally on second were tagged first, even though he was the lead runner, he would be out because the dropped fly ball forced him to advance to third. If the runner originally on first were tagged first, the call there would be safe because the dropped fly ball forced him to advance to second and that is where he is standing. If the batter were to be tagged first, he is out because the runner originally on first who now would be entitled to second hasn't abandoned that bag by advancing farther than forced by the hit, and the batter/runner, as the trailing runner, is not yet entitled to second base. His legal base is first, and he is not there so he is out.

At any point in this scenario, as long as all three runners hold fast to that base, whenever the batter/runner is tagged, he is out because there is no condition in this play where he can legally be on second base as long as both other runners are on the base as well. If, however, the lead runner has been tagged out, then the runner originally from first steps off the bag and is tagged, he is out. Then and only then would the batter/runner be the legal occupant of second base with two outs because there are no other legal runners on the bases. Totally confused yet?

After first tagging the lead runner out, the second baseman then touches the runner originally on first base but now standing on second. As second is his legal base, he is declared safe. If the second baseman tags first the lead runner and then the batter/runner while all three are standing on the bag, those two runners are out.

Now, had the right fielder caught the ball, the batter

would have been out and touching him would be irrelevant. It would change things for the other two runners. The lead runner would then not be forced to advance and he would be the legal occupant of second base while the runner originally on first would be out regardless of the order in which they are tagged.

And the third fly in the ointment: if the ball were shallow enough to be declared an infield fly, the batter is automatically out whether the ball is caught or not and no runners are forced to advance. If the runner originally on first attempts to return to that base and successfully reaches it before he or the base is tagged, you treat it like a fly ball when the runner left the base early, he is safe. He is not running the bases counterclockwise to confuse the defense but rather to return to his proper base. The runner on second is not forced to advance and may stay on second base just like the coach told him. And the batter is still out.

Do you have a slight throbbing at the base of your skull? Take two aspirin and relax for a moment before continuing. It can give you more than a headache trying to figure this one out on the field.

*   *   *

When a runner has to slide into a base in order to avoid the tag, not only does the umpire have to watch the play closely, he must also continue to watch the players' actions closely. And, by the way, players, I don't care how many times you have seen these big league players sliding into a base headfirst, it's not safe. The ball being thrown to the base for the putout attempt generally is going to be low and at least in the area of the sliding runner. If you are sliding headfirst into such a throw, you could get hit in the head with the ball. You may still have your helmet on (it actually should be worn the entire time you are on the field, but we've seen those same big leaguers 'accidentally' flip the helmet off while circling the bases), and it will protect your head but you are still going to feel that hit. For your own protection, players, slide in feet first. By the way, Little League rules requires it.

With a runner on first base and a two-man umpiring crew with me on the field in the "B" position, the batter hits a slow roller back to the pitcher who picked up the ball and fired it to the second baseman covering the bag. For some reason (and with the younger players, usually even they can't tell you a reason) the second baseman did not just touch the bag with his foot once he received the ball for the force out but rather tried to reach down to tag the runner sliding into the base. The runner saw this and slid in to the back corner of the bag to avoid the putout.

He was successful in his effort and I called him "Safe." However, he had slid with such force, his body was now completely past the base and he was reaching back, maintaining contact seemingly only with the fingertips of his left hand. He needed to have time called in order to stand back up. With a possible play still at first base with the batter/runner, I could not just call time for this player's benefit so I continued to watch him for the request for time.

The defensive player also knew the runner would have to obtain a time out to safely get up from his position on the ground so, as opposed to throwing to first base for the possible out of the batter/runner, he continued to hold his glove on the runner's back as he lay prone on the ground reaching back to the base. To request time from an umpire, a runner needs to either verbally make the request or raise his hand similar to the time gesture the umpire would give him in response. It is a very easy thing to do except, with the fielder's glove with the ball firmly inside still applied to his back, he had to maintain contact with the base while making the request.

Holding the base with his left hand, all he needed to do was raise his right hand, which was by his side, to ask for 'time.' But apparently this runner was left-handed because he started to reach forward with his right hand to grab the bag while raising his left hand to ask for time.

Unfortunately (for him), he let go of the bag with his left hand before grabbing it with his right hand and, with the tag still being applied, I had to call the young man out. The look on his face was like those jigsaw puzzle characters with the big, sad eyes but he knew what he had done and had to accept the call.

It was the coach in the third base dugout who didn't see the release of the bag and now came onto the field to argue the call. How these managers, who are more than a hundred feet away from the play, think they can see it better than an umpire who is less than ten feet away from the action, I will never understand. The runner knew what he had done and walked dejectedly to his bench while the manager continued to rant in defense of the runner I just called safe seconds before only to change my call. He would not listen to the fact that the runner let go of the bag and he even laid down on the ground where the runner had been to show me how the runner was still on the base. Big mistake!

Once he stood up I calmly asked him, "Are you trying to show me up out here that I didn't see the play?"

"You know [expletive deleted] well you didn't see the play. You know he was safe so just admit it."

The one thing in baseball that I do not like to do is throw a player, manager or other participant out of the game. But this guy earned the ejection. Profanity has no place on the kids' baseball field. I know it's something they probably hear every day, maybe even in school, but for two hours a night on my field, I don't want to hear that language and certainly the kids don't need to hear it.

* * *

The batter/runner is permitted to overrun first base. He doesn't have to stop on the bag but can run through it without being put out – within reason.

So many youngsters in the lower age groups want to run to first base and stop because their coaches have told them 'don't leave the bag.'

In the Official Baseball Rules, the word except or exception is stated no fewer than sixteen times so their confusion is very understandable. Unless is used with far more frequency and just adds to the confusion.

With a runner on first and one out already recorded, the ten-year-old batter hit the ball slowly to the shortstop. When the ball reached the fielder (because he didn't charge it like he had been taught), it was too late to put out the runner going to second so instead this fielder threw the ball to first for the batter/runner. The batter/runner reached the bag well before the throw got there and was ruled safe. He did overrun the bag and, about three steps beyond the base, turned to the left to return to the base. The first baseman stepped out to meet him with the ball still firmly in his glove and placed a tag on the runner. As field umpire, I had been in the "B" position with the runner on first and had not moved over to the "C" position because I felt there would be a play at first. It just wasn't the play I was expecting.

I again indicated that he was safe by word and exaggerated action. "But he turned toward second base. He's out." beseeched the fielder as he continued to hold a tag on the runner who had now returned to first base.

The third base coach, in watching this little drama, quietly urged his runner now on second base to head for third. The first baseman was unwilling to give up his argument the batter/runner was out. He continued to hold the tag on him, explaining to me, "He turned to the left. He was heading to second base."

"In my judgment," I began with three safest words an umpire could utter, "while he may have turned to the left, he made no effort to advance to second base." I paused for a moment debating with myself whether to mention this but then decided I would. "However, the other runner is now sitting on third base."

So intent was this fielder on the batter/runner, he had no clue there was even another runner on base. Now this forgotten runner already reached third base safely and was talking with his coach when the first baseman decided to throw across the field to get him out.

The third baseman was not paying any attention to the thrown ball coming over to his side of the field (always know where the ball is and what you are going to do with it if it winds up in your glove) so he made no effort to catch it. I really doubt he even saw it coming. As the ball hit the ground and rolled under a spectator's lawn chair in the dead territory area explained to the managers at the pregame meeting, my umpiring partner loudly announced, "Dead ball! Both runners advance two bases!" He pointed to the runner standing on third base talking with his coach and said, "You get home" indicating home plate at his feet. He then turned to the batter/runner standing safely on first base and by indication awarded him second and third.

The defensive team manager was immediately up off the bench and into the home plate umpire's face. "He just said that runner was not going to second now you give him third! You can't do that."

"Coach," my partner explained in as calm of a tone as he could muster, "when your fielder threw the ball into dead territory" indicating the area where parents were sitting behind third base "all runners are entitled to advance two bases. That's ground rules, remember?"

"But they weren't even trying to advance!" He was right as both runners were firmly on the bases they were intending to stand on, they did get to advance on the errant throw.

The topper of this situation? While the batter/runner was jogging his way over to third base, the first baseman turned to me. "I told you he was going to second base."

As I jogged over the "C" position with a runner on third, I had no comeback at the time but since then have come up with dozens … none of which I will insert here, though.

*   *   *

Carl Kirksey was a very talented youngster who could seemingly fly around the bases before the ball just hit to the clouds fell untouched to the deepest part of right-center field. When I was in my last year of playing youth baseball around age thirteen or so, he was entering his second. At maybe ten years old, this kid was already looking at running track in high school. The problem was that if there was a runner on base in front of him, he had to be careful not to pass him. On more than one occasion he came sliding into home plate with his foot right practically under the butt of the sliding runner previously on second base.

One particular afternoon at Earley's Hill Park, though, he didn't hit the ball as far as he thought and the right fielder got to it quicker than Carl anticipated. The throw went directly to second base and Carl slid into the bag to avoid the tag. It was going to be close but Carl had a good head of speed when he extended his right leg and tucked his left leg under him to catch the bag in full sliding posture. Unfortunately, the cleats on his right shoe caught the canvas bag and stuck as he barreled in behind the foot.

The Good Lord may have designed the anklebone to withstand the pounding of the human body upon it in running while vertical but, in this position, something had to give. And it did. As the throw came in to the shortstop covering the bag, the ankle snapped loudly. Carl screamed in pain as the rest of his body followed the foot into the bag.

The tag went on him and he was safe. When his forward momentum stopped, by reflex he reached down to his foot, as anyone would have, perhaps hoping that action would take away the pain. Obviously, it did not and he rolled off the bag in total pain as the coaches from both benches rushed out to do whatever they could for this young man. However, the fielder continued to hold the tag on his back and the umpire then pounded his fist into the air to call the runner out for being off the base.

Even the defensive manager argued with the umpire but the call was technically correct. Fearful to move Carl but not wanting to wait for an ambulance, one of the parents drove their station wagon onto the field and he was carefully lifted into the back and driven to the hospital.

His baseball for the summer was over. He still came back for the games with a cast on his leg and cheered as much as possible from the lawn chair at the end of the bench.

He's still involved in the Ohio Hot Stove Baseball League in Alliance, once serving as Alliance Chapter League president. Doubtless he still remembers Buck's three questions, though that one day he may not have had all that much fun. But he did come back the next day.

As an umpire I remember that play and have added to my field instructions at home plate to the managers before the game, "In the event of an injury, I'll call 'Time.' You take care of the injury; I'll put the runners where they need to be. We are here for the boys (and girls) and their safety comes first." No coach has ever argued it with me.

* * *

With the explosion of technological devices, it was inevitable such would come to the ball fields. With few exceptions, most fields have eliminated the manually operated scoreboards kids loved to operate, sliding the proper number in the slot for the runs scored that inning. It is not uncommon for lighted scoreboards even at youth league fields to be operated from a laptop computer at the scorer's table. Granted, they don't always keep up with the batter's count but they do serve the purpose of posting the score (hence the name of "scoreboard") and on several fields who the batter is supposed to be by their uniform jersey number.

I believe there is a place for such devices to be used as

well as some places where they should not be in use. There should be no cell phones on the playing field or in the coaches' boxes. The people who are in the coaches' boxes are there to aid the runners and the batter in carrying out their team's game plan. They do this by hand and body signals that their team has designed to communicate with their players. I have found it interesting and fun to try to pick up a team's signs by watching the coaches and the players' reactions to them. Once I've seen a team two or three times during the season and feel I have a grasp on their signs, I might ask the batter, after the third base coach has gone through all his motions, "Now, you got all that?" Some of these batters must believe they are the only ones around the field who can see the signs because of their reactions to my simple question. I really hate to tell them but many other eyes are also watching the coaches for any hint of what the batter or the runners might be intending. So, of course, the coaches have to go through a complete series of signals designed to camouflage the true signals.

There was one team I felt went way overboard in that effort of signals. With runners on first and third, I noticed the coach on first base had his back turned to home plate. With the pitcher about ready to deliver the ball, it was not a safe position for the coach so I called time for his protection.

The coach reacted quickly to my call to him and, as he turned around, I could see he was holding something in his hands. It was a cell phone and he was apparently texting someone. "Ah, Coach," I asked, "we're here to play some baseball. What do you think you're doing?"

Nothing up to that point in time could have prepared me for his response. "I'm texting him the signals," he said indicating the coach on third base. And, when I looked down the third base line, the coach there also had a cell phone out and was apparently reading an incoming text message.

"No, no, no, no, no!" I exclaimed. "We can't have this. You guys have got to put those cell phones away." They appeared shocked at my suggestion (but I wasn't suggesting). "In baseball," I explained, "we have this thing called signals that players and coaches use to communicate with each other."

"But," countered the first base coach (and apparently manager of his team), "I want to make sure he," indicating his coaching partner, "knows what I want."

"So make your signals very clear to understand," I advised.

"But I don't want them"—indicating the opponents' dugout—"to pick them up."

"Looks like you have a problem," I finally observed. "But you're not going to solve it by texting each other. We need your attention on the ball field and the baseball, please. No cell phones in the coaches' boxes," I then announced to both sides. "It's a safety factor and I want to put a stop to it right here, right now."

How they communicated for the rest of the game, I do not know. But I do know there was no more texting from one coaching box to the other. I'm still shaking my head at that one.

*   *   *

Continuing with the presence of cellular devices on the field, there was the most unusual case of a very important telephone call. I have attempted to enforce a personal ground rule of no cell phones and such on the field, but there are some parents who attempt to take on too much in their lives so that one volunteer activity crosses over into another. Such was the case in a ten-and eleven-year-old contest a few years ago.

At the beginning of a half-inning I noticed the coach at first base was facing the field and talking up a storm. The problem was there were no runners on the bases for him to be addressing. As the batter stepped in and I still had my right hand extended for time, I pointed across my body with my left hand to the coach and asked, "Does he do that often?"

The batter looked over where I was pointing and responded to my question with a question (don't you just love that?): "Do what?"

"Talk to himself," I responded.

"Oh," the batter said as he set himself for the pitch, "he's just talking on his cell phone. He's the fire chief and there's a fire somewhere." The batter shrugged it off as if it happened every day, and it may have. "He's probably talking to the commander on site," he concluded.

"Oh, no," I said with a chuckle in my voice. Though I still had my hand up for time, I shouted "time" as I stepped out from behind the catcher and took a couple of steps toward first base. I took my mask off with my left hand and shouted, "Hey, Coach, tell me you're not on your cell phone on the field?" I emphasized the question-statement with the universally accepted signal to my ear with my right hand. He responded with a similarly accepted signal to wait a minute, raising the index finger (as least I think it was the index finger) of one hand, and then turned his back to me while he continued his conversation.

"No, no, Coach," I said to him, "No cell phones on the field." I pointed toward the bench area. "If you must be on the phone, take it over there. If you're here, I need your attention on the game."

Someone from the dugout area said, "He'll just be a minute."

"And we're all supposed to what? Just wait for him?" I inquired, not exactly sure who had spoken. "I don't think so. If he needs to be on the phone, get someone else out here."

The fire chief still had his back turned to me and was seemingly shouting to absolutely no one. He had no phone in his hand as he was gesturing with both his arms so I figured he had a hands-free (isn't that called a Bluetooth?) plugged into his ear. I'm not even sure he realized I was holding up the game just because of him.

An adult stepped out of the dugout and said in a low voice, "We don't have anyone else to go out there."

I knew it would be opening a can of worms but without lowering the volume of my voice one bit, I made a suggestion. "Let one of the kids come out here, then." Immediately, I think every one of the players was on the fence in front of the dugout with a hand up stretched shouting, "Let me do it. Pick me. I can do it, Mr. Adams. Pick me."

Coach Adams gave me a look as if to say, 'Now look what you've done.' Just then the first base coach-fire chief entered into the conversation, telling Coach Adams, "Sorry, I've got to go. They need me over there."

Now the remaining coach was in a pickle. With no other adults, he would either have to have one of the players in the coach's box or leave it empty. He decided to put one of the players there. "He needs a batting helmet on in there," I advised as I turned to head back to home plate. "And I need him to stay in the box so I can tell the runner from the coach."

As I returned to the home plate area to resume the game (unknown to me the pitcher had continued to throw to the catcher during this time, which was good because it kept his arm loose but bad because he was tiring out the arm with all those extra throws), the batter once again set himself in the batter's box. I put on the mask, checked my indicator to be sure it was all zeroes and then shouted down to the youngster in the first base coach's box, "You ready?" He indicated he was. "Pay attention. Keep your eyes on the ball and no showboating." He nodded his head in agreement. A quick look to the adult coach at third base to be sure he was ready and I returned my attention to the three players in front of me—pitcher, catcher and batter.

"Okay," I shouted, "Play ball!"

I could hear the car siren of the fire chief's vehicle sounding as he left the parking lot as the first pitch came in for strike one.

* * *

In the older divisions, fifteen-to eighteen-year-old, with a two-man umpiring crew, I was behind the plate with no outs and runners on first and second. The field umpire was in the "C" position, on the infield grass between second and third. The batter lifted a pop-up to mid-right field, too deep for an Infield Fly Rule call but not so deep that it couldn't reasonably be caught.

By all rights the field umpire should have held his position in order to handle the catch-no catch call and I had the runners if they tried to advance after the catch. As he told me afterward, "I just forgot my assignment and backed up to cover the runners." It all worked out okay but there was a moment.

I moved out from behind the plate in foul territory toward third base so I could see the runners tag up and the catch being made. What I didn't expect to see was my field umpire moving toward the inside "B" position between first and second to watch the runners and leaving the catch to me.

As I watched the right fielder set his feet to make the catch and throw into the infield, I could also see the runner at first had set himself to advance upon the fielder touching the ball. But the runner's foot was off the bag. It was propped against a pile of dirt maybe four or five inches away from the bag that he doubtless, without looking, thought was the base.

When the right fielder made the catch for out number one, my field umpire made no indication of out or not so I had to make the call and then looked over to the runner at first to see him moving toward second base. Without taking his eyes off the action in front of him as the right fielder threw the baseball to second base, he shouted over his shoulder in my direction, "You got third base, Michael."

I wasn't sure if he was asking or telling but, as he was the senior umpire, I responded, "I've got third if he goes but you've got both ends of the rundown."

He hadn't thought of that. As the runner on second gave no indication of trying to advance, I moved into the infield for a better position if I could help in the rundown that was developing between first and second. I saw the catcher move up the line to back up first base and worried that his leaving home plate unprotected would encourage the runner on second to attempt to score. Fortunately he continued to hold fast to second base as the defensive fielders tossed the ball back and forth, with each throw shortening the distance available for the runner to move.

Then it happened. The ball got away from the first baseman and the runner advanced to second without ever having retouched first base As the catcher picked up the errant ball before it rolled into dead territory (which would have allowed all runners to advance two bases without jeopardy of being put out), the runner originally on second was now joined at the bag by the runner previously on first. Now keep in mind by the book the trailing runner cannot legally advance to an occupied base until that runner has vacated it either by legally advancing to another base himself or being put out. Fortunately my umpiring partner was aware of this and therefore did not call the runner safe at second base. In fact, being no play on the runner, there was no reason for him to make a call of any kind. So he didn't.

In the heat of the moment, the runner who had been standing on second base didn't think of that. Instead, with another runner now occupying second base with him, he felt he had to vacate the bag and move toward third.

The alert catcher threw the baseball to the waiting third baseman who applied the tag on the approaching runner well off the bag and I rang him up for the second out.

At this point a coach from the defensive team dugout behind me was shouting to his third baseman, "He left early. Throw it to first."

The fielder actually turned and asked, "What?" So coach again told him to throw the ball to first. With the catcher still covering the base, the ball came back to him and he stepped on the bag to make the appeal.

The appeal was completely legal as the action was all in one continuous play and the ball was still alive. But the field umpire to whom the appeal was made didn't see that the tag up or lack thereof was not on the bag, apparently having a bad angle on the play. He ruled the player safe.

It was at this point that the coach came out of the dugout and asked for time as he approached me. "You saw it," he said. "He wasn't anywhere near the bag."

I would have agreed with him but instead had to tell him, "He made the call, sir," indicating my umpiring partner. "Go speak with him." It is something we always try to mention in the pregame ground rules' meeting with the managers: "If you have a question with a call, please go to the umpire that made the call to discuss your differences."

"But you saw it," he continued. "You can overrule him." He was right but I had to be asked by the umpire that made the original call before I could offer an opinion. Like the third ghost in *A Christmas Carol*, I continued to stand there silently with my outstretched arm pointing to the other official.

The coach finally moved over to my field partner who was still standing behind the pitcher's area. "He didn't tag up," I could hear the coach tell the umpire. "He saw it. Ask him." The comment now referred to me as I was walking back to the home plate area. For some reason the catcher was still standing on first base with the ball still in his mitt, perhaps thinking the longer he stood there, the more convincing his coach's argument would be perceived. Seriously, there are times when it is very difficult to figure out what these players are thinking. But he continued to stand there, foot on the bag, ball still in his mitt.

As I looked up, I heard the field umpire shout "Time!" The call wasn't necessary as I had already granted time as the coach was coming on to the field. My partner was pointing to me, palm up, asking for a conference.

Now I may be giving away a trade secret here but when one umpire motions to another concerning an appeal of a call, if he points with a finger, the conference is generally just for show as he just wants to appease the coach by discussing with another umpire before repeating his previous call. The finger pointing means, "I saw the play clearly; I just need you to back me up." If the hand is open with the palm up, he is seriously asking for help. And this was a case where he knew he had been out of position to see the play and wanted to see if I thought I had a better view of the situation.

I indicated for him to meet me between the mound and first base away from the fielders and coach. As we met, putting my hand over my mouth to prevent any lip reading (Does it happen? Oh, yes, so the action of protection is very much advised) and, without pointing, I said, "You see that mound of dirt there away from first base?" Without nodding, he said he did. "That's where he tagged up. He never touched the bag."

"Okay, so he's out?"

"That's your call to make," I said quietly, "but, since you asked, that's how I saw it."

It may have taken all of five to seven seconds and the conference was done. We separated as the field umpire announced the runner was out for leaving the base early. There was no argument from the offensive bench because they had seen the same thing I had.

Triple play.

123

*   *   *

When my older sister, Lucindia, became involved in a Woman's Slow Pitch Softball League, a pastry shop in town, known as Sugar 'n' Spice, sponsored her team. As this was a league for women, profanity was not to be permitted on the field. However, the word sugar took on a whole new meaning for a few summers in Alliance. Obviously Lu was not one of the girls to write batter as her desired position. Rather, she would play almost any position on the field except catcher or pitcher. She was the biggest tomboy I had ever seen in my life; even the neighborhood bully backed down when he'd threatened one of her brothers. So, playing baseball (or softball) was not unexpected.

On this particular afternoon she was playing third base in a close contest with their major rivals. With runners on first and second and one out, the batter hammered a line drive into left field and the runners were off with the sound of the bat. The left fielder was quick to get the ball and threw it in to Lu at third base in hopes of getting the force-out. Sis had her right foot blocking the infield side of the bag from the sliding runner as she set herself to receive the throw. Even if the throw was late, the runner couldn't make it to the bag because of her foot in the way.

This little fact didn't stop the runner from trying, though. The ball and the runner arrived at practically the same instant (and ties do not always go to the runner) but the runner was wearing rubber spike shoes with metal tips for running traction and was called out. Lu caught herself before she fell on the runner but contact was made with her ankle and she took a couple of steps toward the shortstop position to catch her balance and walk off any sting from the slide.

It may have been softball but the Sugar 'n' Spice Sweeties wore long pants for uniforms with baseball stirrup socks and white tube socks beneath. Lu stopped about four steps away from the third base bag, leaned down to lower her socks and examined her right ankle. There was a cut on the skin and little blood but nothing to take her out of the game. However, when she pulled the sock back up, looking at the material, her reaction was such you would have thought a bench-clearing brawl was about to break out. She looked at the runner who was beginning to walk away from the bag towards her bench with a stare that would have stopped the Chicago Bears defensive line. "She tore my sock!" Lu screamed. The girl stopped in mid-step and turned to look at Lucindia. I couldn't tell you if the look on her face was one of fear or amusement but at least she was smart enough not to say a word before continuing her now somewhat hasty retreat to her bench and the security of her teammates. "She tore my sock!" Lucindia shouted again. Never mind the cut on her ankle and the little bit of blood. Cuts heal and the blood can be washed off. But the hole in the sock would require sewing to repair. And this was the major concern of my sister. Now mind you, it wasn't that she couldn't sew, but this was unnecessary damage to the uniform.

"There's a hole in my sock!"

*   *   *

I mentioned before the object of the game is to score more runs than your opponent. And to score more runs you need to have your players on offense safely advance through the bases in order. I've also mentioned the number of times that except and unless are used within the rules. It can be very confusing at times. And when you attempt to apply those rules to varying ages of youth, sometimes their understanding may be a little different than intended.

With two outs in the bottom of the fifth inning of an eleven-and twelve-year-old's contest, the score was tied. The home team just needed to get one of the two runners on second and third safely across home plate to win the game. But, of course, it couldn't have been just as easy as that.

125

Life Behind The Mask

As the only umpire for this game, I feared we would be looking at a tie game, called because of time limits (no inning could start after 8:30 on a school night and we were already at 8:40) and I knew it wasn't easy to arrange a date in the future to get both teams and myself back together to finish the contest. The umpire could be different for, in fact, I had filled in a few times as umpire to finish the last inning or so of a game, but finding an open date for both teams could be difficult.

The batter was a small player who didn't have much strength in his swing. With no force-out available, the infielders were pulled in to cut down the play at the plate. The outfielders were at normal depth as, with two outs already recorded, there would be no tag ups to score after a fly out. This had all the makings of a very dramatic finish. But, I get ahead of myself.

The little batter swung at the first two pitches, only managing to foul off the second pitch back to the backstop. The third pitch was a teaser curve ball just off the plate for ball one. The fourth pitch, though, must have gotten away from the pitcher because it was right on the outside corner of the plate, belt high and begging to be hit. And the batter obliged it for a game-winning single right over second base.

The batter started a slow trot to first base and then, after four or five steps, turned around to watch the runner from third cross the plate to win the game. He then stopped and returned to home plate to join in the celebration.

As the defensive team left the field and headed for their third base dugout, the center fielder picked up the batted ball and started his own trot but toward first base. The winning home team was already beginning to gather at first base for the usual across the field congratulations when the fielder reached the bag with the ball in his glove. "Blue," he shouted at me, "the batter never reached first base."

Attention now focused on me, as it usually did when

126

something unusual like this would happen. I waited for it and then declared, "You are correct. He did not reach first base. The batter is out! That is the third out of the inning! No runs score!"

The winning team manager went ballistic. "What do you mean? He doesn't have to reach first base. The runner on third already scored. The game is over."

"Coach, the runner on third was not forced to advance. The batter does have to reach first base before the ball gets there or else he is out. Just like any ordinary play. It was obvious he never got within twenty feet of the bag before he came back to home plate." I explained to him in as calm a voice as I could manage. "Sorry, Coach. He's out and we've still got a tie game."

"No! No! He's not out!" the manager continued to shout as some of his players stepped out onto the field to exchange high-fives and handshakes with the other team. They were satisfied with my ruling, as the players usually are. It was the adults who couldn't understand. "I'm gonna protest this. You're a joke of an umpire!"

It's not something I hadn't heard before and I've never let it bother me. In this case, the game was over for the night by curfew so I turned away from him and headed for the backstop to collect my water bottle and head for home. Unfortunately, this manager wasn't so willing to give up. As I bent over to pick up my water bottle, I could see him approaching me from behind. Just as I stood up, he grabbed me on the shoulder and spun me around so I would be facing him. He continued into his tirade that I was a bad umpire and I didn't know the rules and he would see to it I never umpired another game in my life.

"Coach," I said coolly, "I suggest you calm down and think about what you just did."

"Oh," he said, "what are you gonna do? Punch me?"

I have never and would never lay a hand on a manager in anger. It sets a bad example for the kids and would destroy my credibility in my role as an impartial adjudicator of the rules. It is because of that position as an umpire that under the laws of several states amateur umpires are protected under the same laws as police officers. And, as you well know, striking a police officer is just not permitted. So when this manager grabbed me and spun me around, he was already in more trouble than he ever could have imagined.

I did not call the police but it just so happened that the son of a local city police officer was playing at one of the other fields and the father was in attendance. Quickly he was at my field and by my side. "You need some help here, Blue?" he asked me in that way that police officers surely have been trained to speak.

"Game's over. I'm just trying to leave." I honestly informed him.

The officer turned his attention to the manager and asked, "You got a problem with that?"

"He's an a**hole," the manager said motioning toward me.

The officer turned to me and said, "Your call, Blue. I can take him down or just make a report of it." He seemed like he really wanted to put this guy in handcuffs and toss him in the back of a squad car and he just wanted me to give him permission.

The last thing I wanted to do was to embarrass this manager any more than he'd already done himself and then have to make a police report at this time of night. "Just get me to my car and give me your card. I'll give you a call tomorrow," I suggested.

"I can do that," he responded and we started walking together off the field. Unfortunately our path took us toward that team's dugout. Before I realized it, before I could explain it to the officer, I was being led right into the lion's den. The players, coaches and spectators all parted to allow us through when one of the parents leaned in and said, "Good call, Blue. I was wondering about that myself."

You know, it's things like that that can make the whole night worthwhile. The kids know I'm out there for them. But when a parent speaks up and realizes just what the umpires have to go through on a regular basis, it reaffirms my trust in them as parents and as citizens.

I did call the officer the next morning but never filed an official report with the police although I did call the chapter's umpire-in-chief once I got home just to let him know what had happened. Three weeks later the game was resumed on a Saturday afternoon. Honestly I can't tell you who won but I do know that manager was not at the game. I had heard the chapter suspended him for his conduct directed at an umpire. I hate to get people in trouble for their own stupidity but I'd hate it more if somewhere down the line another umpire or even a player suffered physical injury at the hands of this individual because I didn't speak up. It's only a game—but the kids are watching.

*   *   *

As kids when we would play our own version of street baseball, bases would be assigned as the street light pole for first base, the sewer manhole cover for second base and the rear fender of the Ford parked on the street as third base. Of course for some reason as soon as Mr. Glasser realized we were using his car for third base, he came out to move it. Then we'd have to come up with something else to use for third base. Home plate was drawn with chalk on the street.

When we would progress to playing in league games at Earley's Hill fields, the bases were actual official canvas bases with two straps across the base connected to a metal stake driven into the ground. These were more permanent bases, but not always entirely permanent.

In a "G" League contest on Earley's Hill #1 field, the batter hit a solid blast into right field that was not handled cleanly by the right fielder. Just as sure as the batter/runner was that he would stretch this to a double, the defensive player was sure he would cut him down at second base. As both the ball and the runner approached the base, everyone could tell it would be a close play.

The batter/runner began his slide and made it to the bag just a fraction of a second before the ball smacked into the second baseman's glove. As he moved down to apply the tag to the batter/runner's leg, the second base bag broke loose from its straps and headed off about ten feet into left field.

The runner, realizing he was no longer in contact with the base and the fielder was applying a tag to his leg, attempted to get up and regain contract with the base. The fielder who applied the tag on the runner was now urging the home plate umpire who had come out to cover the play complete with his big balloon chest protector to call the runner out. Instead, though, like a football referee explaining that the ground caused the fumble by the ball carrier, the umpire was repeatedly pointing to the ground where the base should have been and was saying, "The bases aren't stationary. The runner is safe. The bases aren't stationary. The runner is safe."

The managers from both teams came out to retrieve the errant base and reconnect it with the triangle loop on the top of the stake and tie it up firm so as not to come loose again. But you must admit it was a comical scene of the runner trying to get to the base in left field while the fielder was trying to hold a tag on him.

*   *   *

Baseball is a game divided into segments of equal opportunities for each team to score runs. Baseball is the only one of the major sports whose length is not determined by a clock but rather by innings. Obviously the visiting team bats first and therefore has the first opportunity to score. In baseball, you cannot score if you are not up to bat. As defense, you can only prevent the other team from scoring. The defensive team has nine players on the field to accomplish this while at most the offensive team can have four players at a time on the field to score runs. When the defensive team has recorded three outs against the offensive team, they switch sides and do it all over again. The defense becomes offense and the offense becomes defense. Depending on the rules and the ages of the players, games in various youth leagues can last for 5, 6, 7 or 9 innings at least. If the score is tied at the end of a regulation number of innings, additional innings shall be played to determine the winning team. Each team will have an equal opportunity to score runs to win the game.

After six innings of the eleven-and twelve-year-old's contest, the score was tied. In the top of the seventh, the visiting team went ahead by two runs.

As the home team left the field between innings, their players were down. They felt they already lost the game. But their manager was anything but defeated. "They're done!" he told his players. "They've had their last bats. They can't score any more runs. We can. We can score all the runs we need. So let's get started." He was clapping his hands and giving encouragement to his players. And he was 100% right.

I never thought of it in that way before (there are often times during the course of a game I actually forget who is the home team; I am so wrapped up in the mechanics of the game the details escape me), but when the visiting team takes the field for the bottom of that last inning or an extra inning, they can't score any more runs without going to another inning of play. All they can do is their best efforts to prevent the home team from scoring enough runs to win the game. And, if the home team is behind at that time, they can either play for the win or just to get enough runs to force another complete inning in order to try it all over again.

There's been games go into the eleventh and twelfth

innings with the tie having been broken and then re-tied three times or more before finally deciding a winner. This is where the scorekeepers become a very important part of the game and having them close to the backstop is vital to an umpire. He needs to know the score and they need to know if the runner just crossing the plate as part of the third out play would count. I encourage the scorekeepers to check with each other frequently during the course of the game to make sure they have the same score. If they don't, that needs to be brought to my attention immediately so we can see who might have made a mistake when and correct it. There have been times, I will admit, that my waving off a run that failed to score properly may be viewed as indicating a runner at home plate was safe and therefore should be counted. That is where this umpire's loud voice comes into play to indicate a wave off a run and say, "That run does *not* count," followed by "the third out was already made" or some such explanation. My brother contends I give too many explanations and should offer them only if asked. This is an area of the game where we agree to disagree. He officiates at the upper age groups where the players and coaches should know the rules. In the youngest of players and greenest of coaching staffs, I feel an explanation can only improve the quality and understanding of the game, if not on that day, at least in the future.

The Pitcher

To be a pitcher in baseball requires, among other talents, the ability to throw the baseball exactly where you want and with the type of pitch you intend to throw at the time. Pitchers have several legal pitches from which to choose. Typically they have fastball, curve, change-up, and maybe a slider. Variations may also include a side-arm pitch of each or maybe even a submarine style. Some may also have developed a knuckle ball, but my opinion is such a pitch can actually do more damage to the harm than good for a pitcher. For a ten-year-old boy to throw these basic pitches with the ability necessary is not an easy task. It also requires being able to see and understand the signals of the catcher for the pitches.

Generally the manager will signal to the catcher what pitch he wants thrown to that batter. This is done by a series of touches to various parts of the upper body or face that the catcher will interpret from the prearranged code. He then signals to the pitcher by placing his bare hand between his knees while in the catching position. In the simplest terms, he will hold down one, two, three or four fingers and then tap either leg to indicate either right side or left side of the plate for location. If this pitch is to be up around the batter's elbows, he may lift his thumb upwards. If the pitch is to be down low, he may flatten his hand palm down and lower it in front of him. All of this is done in less than three seconds.

If the pitcher understands the signal and agrees with the pitch, he'll nod his head. If either he disagrees with the selection or doesn't understand, he shake his head no. If he wants the catcher to go through the sign again, he may take his bare hand and indicate a small winding motion.

Okay, got all that? Understand the pitcher is anywhere from forty-six feet for the youngest player up to the high school distance of sixty feet six inches from the back corner of home plate. And the pitcher must be able to see all of this when the catcher is trying to hide the signals from the batter, the runners and opposing coaches. He may do so by giving multiple signals with an activator signal just before the actual signal for the pitch. There are so many variations of the signals and, being behind the catcher, I have no way of knowing what they are.

The catcher went through the signals and the pitcher had a blank look on his face. From my perspective behind the catcher, I could see this ten-year-old didn't understand what he was expected to throw. He motioned for the catcher to run through the signs again. So the catcher did. No change from the pitcher. He blinked a couple of times as the catcher apparently began the process a third time. Finally the pitcher straightened up and said "Huh?"

As I laughed at the situation, I told the catcher, "Just go out there and tell him what you want." This is a fun game.

*   *   *

"Baseball is for boys and softball is for girls." Now that is *not* my idea but the general perception of many people involved in organized youth baseball. Many groups that organize baseball leagues have fought tooth and nail to prevent girls from being able to play on the same field as the boys. And leagues that I umpired in were the same way for many years until they were finally required to enroll girls in order to continue using the city's recreational fields. So adamant they were against it that they would actually establish a girls' softball league just to have equity for the girls to prevent them from being able to play baseball.

But, as they all knew would happen, girls were finally allowed in organized youth baseball. Personally I enjoy seeing the girls playing on the same field because generally they are more coordinated and can field and hit better than the boys, a fact that the male parents of male children would never admit except I have three daughters and no sons so I know better.

When the boys get to the high school, there may only be

two or three teams in a small-sized city so teams must travel to other communities for games. In a league for ages sixteen and over this team had a female pitcher. In fact, during the school year she pitched fast-pitch softball. Fast-pitch softball is one game I would never umpire because the pitching mound is like forty-three feet from home plate and that twelve-inch yellow softball can come in at speeds of more than sixty to eighty miles an hour. That means the batter has to start her swing practically before it leaves the pitcher's hand. And there is nothing soft about that ball.

Top of the first inning and Carol's team was on the field. During her warm-up pitches, her motion was that of a normal baseball pitcher. However, I had seen her warming up behind the dugout before the game and knew she could also throw the 9¼-inch circumference baseball in her normal fast-pitch softball delivery, knee high.

Warm-up pitches complete, the catcher threw the baseball down to second base as I cleaned off home plate. "Batter up!"

The young man stepped into the batter's box as I put my mask on and got down behind the catcher. Carol was standing on the mound with her right foot on the rubber and the ball in her right hand. Everybody was ready. "Play ball," I instructed. The pitcher looked over to her coach and paying seemingly no attention to the batter. He took a practice swing and then set the bat on his shoulder.

A second or two passed and no one moved. Then suddenly Carol's right hand dropped to her side, she straightened to home plate and delivered an underhand fastball pitch to the batter that never rose more than three inches above his knee. It smacked into the catcher's mitt.

The amazed batter turned to me. "What was that?" he asked.

"You'd better get used to it, son," I responded as I raised my right hand, "because that was strike one," emphasizing the last two words for the spectators and scorekeepers.

He was dumbfounded. Not having watched her off-field warm-ups, he had no idea what to expect. As the catcher threw the ball back to Carol, I advised the batter, "You'd better get ready, son. You don't want to get struck out by a girl." I did my best to suppress a sinister chuckle but I fear I was not entirely successful.

It occurred to him what I had just said. He jumped out of the batter's box like someone just set it on fire. To cover up his reaction, he looked down at his third base coach for a sign. And the coach gave him the best guidance he could: the coach shrugged his shoulders and, with his hands, offered the batter to get back into the box and get ready.

The batter looked back at me as if asking for help. Holding up his trembling hand, he asked, "Time, please, Blue?" I granted it and held my hand up palm outward to indicate to the fielders that time was called.

The batter stepped in and ground his toes into the loose soil to dig in for the pitch. He continued to hold his hand up to me until he was sure he was ready for the pitch.

Dropping my hand, I indicated to Carol, "Play ball."

The second pitch was almost exactly where the first had been and I dutifully called it: "Strike two." On the third pitch this young man was able to make contact but only a weak grounder to the third baseman who promptly threw to first for out number one.

In the four and two-thirds innings Carol pitched that day, I was told she had five strikeouts and did not allow a hit out of the infield or a runner past second base. It was the only time all season I saw her pitch but it was well worth it for the amazement on that young boy's face.

*   *   *

We are constantly battling with the pitchers to hurry up on their between inning warm-up pitches. On fields with no lights in the Ohio summertime, it can be light until nearly nine o'clock but that doesn't mean the game has to last three and a half hours. On an overcast night, it can be getting dark around eight o'clock or so and I have had to call a good many games on account of darkness.

Well, one game I had many years ago the first inning gave me the impression I was not in for a marathon contest. After the pitcher completed his warm-ups and I had brushed off the plate, I called for the batter to step in. "Play ball," I shouted and play they did.

The first pitch was just below the belt on the batter and over the outside corner. The batter lifted the ball to left field and I swear the player didn't have to move a step to make the catch for the first out. The second batter hit the first pitch as a grounder to the third baseman who promptly threw across the field for the second out. Two pitches. The third batter followed suit on the grounder to third and in just over a minute the top half of the inning was done.

After the eight warm-up pitches for the visiting team's pitcher, we were ready to do this for the home team. The first batter required two pitches before he grounded out to the second baseman for the first out. The second batter hit a first-pitch line driven the right back to the pitcher for the second out. He didn't even bother throwing the ball around among the infielders but just set straight about getting ready to pitch to the next batter.

The third batter let his first pitch go for ball one but swung on top of the second pitch resulting in a weak grounder to the third baseman for the last out of the inning.

I looked at my watch to see it was only 6:03. We finished the first complete inning in less than five minutes. Although someone would have to score a run, at this rate we could be done with a seven-inning game before seven o'clock. But you know it didn't happen that way.

*   *   *

When I was a youngster and a player myself, we had a young black pitcher who was very good at his position. At the age of ten, Johnny Holly was probably five foot tall and maybe 150 pounds. His pitching motion told you what kind of a night we could expect. Being a left-handed pitcher, he would raise his right leg in the wind-up position. If the foot came up to his waist, he didn't have his stuff. If the foot was chest high, it was going to be a good night. But if that foot came up over his head, he was unhittable. I've seen innings where he threw only nine pitches to three batters. Each of them a fastball, each right in the middle of the strike zone, and each smacked soundly into the catcher's mitt.

But there was one night when the leg was about waist high and we feared this was going to be a long night. We were the visitors and so we batted first. No runs, one hit and a runner left on second. Then Johnny took the mound. His warm-up pitches were okay. The leg came up to about his waist and the baseball lacked the pop into the catcher's mitt that we would liked to have heard. But, hey, they were only the warm-up pitches. You don't want your pitcher wasting his good stuff on the warm-ups.

The first batter stepped and Johnny began his pitching motion. The leg went up no higher than the waist. The first batter walked on five pitches. The second batter also got a free pass on just four throws. The manager, my father, Buck, went out to talk with him. What was discussed we'll never know, but the next batter also walked on four pitches.

Bases loaded, no outs and Johnny was not in his groove. A second trip to the mound by the coaching staff in the same inning required the changing of the pitcher and I could not remember any time when Johnny was pulled in the first inning. Buck stayed with him.

The fourth batter came to the plate and Johnny suddenly changed. The leg went up over his head and when the ball came down, the pitch smacked into the catcher's glove right in the middle of the plate. The next two pitches followed for the first strike out. The next batter stepped in probably more confused than he ever before in his young life. His confusion was soon irrelevant as, in three pitches, he was returning to the after never lifted the bat from his shoulder. And likewise was the sixth batter of the inning. Johnny was so much on fire that night this ten-year-old youngster deliberately walked the first three batters only to strike out the next three on three pitches each.

Top of the second we collected four hits and two runs. When Johnny took the mound for the bottom of the second inning, he began by throwing three pitches outside of the strike zone. "Johnny," yelled Buck from the bench area, "don't you dare do that again."

He didn't but there was no doubt to anyone at the field he could if he wanted to for the entire seven innings. Johnny was a joy to watch and he loved to have an audience. Johnny is now a minister in the Southern Baptist faith and still loves an audience, only now he pitches for the Lord.

* * *

I have mentioned elsewhere that very few youth teams actually have five pitchers. Generally speaking few have more than maybe three pitchers. They may have four or even five players who will throw from the pitcher's mound, but their ability to consistently aim for and hit the strike zone is suspect at best.

As of a few years ago the rules governing how frequently a pitcher may be used were changed in Little League baseball. It had been based on the number of innings the youngster threw to determine how much rest he must have before pitching again. If a pitcher threw more than four innings' worth of work (and the rule had been if he threw one pitch of an inning, he was charged with a complete inning—no thirds of an inning), there must be at least three calendar days of rest before returning to the mound. Less than four innings required only one calendar day of rest.

Because the number of pitches thrown in an inning was inconsistent (remember the story about the short inning where only eight pitches were thrown combined by both teams?), leadership decided to establish a standard based on the number of pitches thrown regardless of the number of innings. Fewer than 20 pitches required no specific number of days of rest.

A pitcher under the age of ten may throw no more than seventy-five pitches in one game. Eleven-to twelve-year-olds may throw no more than eighty-five pitches and those thirteen to sixteen are limited to ninety-five pitches in a game. (And I seriously had a rookie scorekeeper ask me if the pitches thrown between innings counted toward that limit. For the record, no, they do not. Those are called warm-up pitches. However, and she later asked to clarify this point, as well, if a batter fouls off a pitch after two strikes, those pitches do count. They just don't add to the batter's count). If the player throws more than sixty pitches in one game, he may not return to the mound in a game condition for three calendar days. Throwing between forty-one and sixty pitches will require two calendar days. Youngsters throwing between twenty-one and forty pitches in one game must rest for one calendar day. Since most teams play on either Monday and Thursday or Tuesday and Friday, pitchers can pitch back to back games if it's handled right. In Florida, Wednesdays are always left open for church night except during postseason tournaments and Saturdays are designated for make-up games. Please understand I am not encouraging youngsters to pitch back-to-back games, but it is possible. The only problem would be if a make-up game were scheduled that could interfere with that schedule.

Concerning that maximum number of pitches portion of the rule, there is an exception to that limit. If the pitcher reaches the maximum level during an at-bat, then he may (but is not required to unless for the first batter of an inning) complete pitching for that batter's turn regardless of how many additional pitches would be required without penalty but must be removed from the mound immediately following that batter's at-bat. That player is not permitted to pitch again before a three-calendar-day rest. He may play other positions on the field during that time; in fact, because of the 'every player must play' rule, he is required to play at least six consecutive defensive outs and have at least one at-'bat in each game during that three-calendar day rest if any that he attends of his team's games.

Before every season the managers and the umpires are provided with new Little League Rulebooks and must sign a statement page acknowledging that they have received the rulebook and have read it. Of course every manager and umpire signs the statement but it is known as a fact that very few managers actually read the rulebook. If they did, there wouldn't be so many arguments—er, I mean disagreements—with the umpires about how a specific rule is enforced. The one concerning a pitcher exceeding the allowed number of pitches is an example of one misunderstood by many parties on both sides of the argument.

With a runner on first and two outs in the inning, a twelve-year-old pitcher reached the eighty-five-pitch limit mark with the second pitch to the batter. By the rule, he would be permitted to complete that batter's turn without violating the limit. However, on the third pitch to the batter, the runner on first attempted to steal second and was thrown out by the catcher for the third out. Since the batter didn't complete his turn at bat, he would lead off the next inning with a count of no balls and no strikes. Since the pitcher was throwing to that batter and did not complete that batter's at-bat, is that same pitcher allowed to start the next inning with the same batter even though he has now exceeded the allowed number of pitches? I e-mailed about thirty other Little League umpires and managers to ask then that very question. Of those responding, not quite a third of them said, "Yes, the same pitcher can come back to finish that batter's turn at bat."

If they had read the rulebook, it clearly stated the pitcher may exceed the maximum limit under three circumstances only. Those are until: (1) The batter is put out, (2) The batter reaches base safely, or (3) The third out of the half-inning is made. So, sorry guys. The pitcher would be done for the day as soon as the third out of the half-inning was made. As one of the respondents put it, for a player of such age, the manager shouldn't allow that situation to occur too often for the player's safety. Wow! Someone was thinking of the player's safety.

*   *   *

Just as much as the offensive team members must communicate with one another during the course of a game, so must the defensive team have clandestine communications among themselves. The obvious point of such is between the catcher and the pitcher for signaling the pitches. But there are other players on the field who must also know the plan for an intended play. With a runner on first who might steal second, the catcher needs to know who will be covering the bag. Sometimes the message is openly stated as either the shortstop or the second baseman saying, "I've got second." In the younger kids' contests, the manager or a coach might yell out from the dugout to tell them who should be covering the bag for the throw.

For a pick-off play to first base, the same level of communication needs to be conveyed between the pitcher and the first baseman as well as the right fielder (to back up an overthrow) and the second baseman (should the runner break for the steal).

With runners on first and third, the play becomes a little more complex in the youth leagues. If the runner on first tries to steal second, a throw down from the catcher could allow the runner on third to come home. But not to throw to second puts two runners in potential scoring position. The offensive team's idea is to have the runner from first break late to disrupt the catcher's throw back to the pitcher and possibly allow both runners to advance safely.

Different teams would have different methods of indicating a special play. Some might have the catcher step in front of home plate and give hand and body signals to the infielders. Others might have a word or phrase indicator for the fielders. I had one team where the catcher would shout out something to the infielders to let them know if a special play was on. Now, just so I might have a heads-up as to what might be happening as the only umpire for most contests, I would try to pick up the signals during the season. But, for this one team, I could not understand what the catcher was saying. It never seemed to be the same thing twice.

Finally, during one game I mentioned to the coach that I had no clue of their defensive signals. He, of course, responded that was good and offered to tell me them later.

After the game, while signing my scorecard, he asked me what I thought the play calls were. I explained it seemed to me the catcher was calling something different each time and I asked him if they changed the call every inning or something. "Not quite," he responded, "but kind of. What do you think he was saying?"

"One time it sounded like 'tomatoes.' Another time was it 'peaches'? And another, 'tuna'?" I said. "I hate to say it but he was making me hungry." I usually won't have dinner before heading to the field for a game so by the end of the contest, around eight o'clock or later, I am getting rather hungry anyway.

The coach chuckled as he handed me the signed scorecard. "Well, it wasn't 'tomatoes,'" he said. "Probably 'potatoes.' But you should have the idea there." I thought for a moment before admitting I had no clue. "Since he never made a throw, it might have been hard to figure out," the coach finally conceded. "If he said a vegetable, like 'potato' or 'corn,' if the runner on first went, he'd throw to the shortstop. If he said a fruit, like 'apples' or 'peaches,' the throw would go to second base."

It was brilliant! And certainly a code no average ten-year-old or opposing manager (or umpire for that matter) could understand or decipher. But the "tuna," if that's what it was?

"If he said a fish, if either runner went, he would throw to third and get ready for a rundown." Very complex, totally undetectable and apparently very effective. I never had the team again that year so I don't know if the manager changed his signals after explaining them to me, but if he had gone to such lengths before I wouldn't doubt that he had.

Many years ago when I played ball (and remember I was the catcher sometimes), before the pitch to the plate, the play was called to the fielders as "Heinz 57." It was just to alert the other fielders of the runners' situation. It was certainly nothing as complex as the previous signals. The idea was the play had a little bit of everything to it. If the runner on first broke for second, the catcher's throw would go to the shortstop that had advanced to the infield grass to back-up the throw back to the pitcher. From there, he could throw back to the plate if the runner on third tried to advance, to second base if there was no play at home but possibly one at second (although that was seldom), or just lob the ball back to the pitcher if there were no plays at all.

In Florida, I had a team whose signal word from the bench was "nachos." That just meant for the players to be aware of the placement of the runners. It wasn't a call for a play. At least none that I was aware of.

The worst results of these gadget plays were that either somebody would throw the ball away or someone would not catch it and the ball would scoot away from a fielder, allowing the runners to advance and even score. It is the defense's job to stop the other team from scoring, but there are times their very efforts to accomplish have the opposite result. Teams need to practice their plays so they can properly perform them when needed.

I wonder why the signal words seemed to often involve food. Maybe because the defensive team intended to eat up the runners on the bases?

*   *   *

Not all umpire's stories are positive. Not all have happy endings. But they do have lessons to be taught or laughs to share. I have had two instances with wild pitches and passed balls that fall under the not-positive category but I'll tell them here.

The first was during my third or fourth year of umpiring. This was a game of nine-and ten-year-olds and between two teams as absolutely opposite as you could get. Team A always had their proper batters ready to go and weren't afraid to swing at close pitches, even if they might not be in the strike zone. Defensively, they were in position and knew what they were going to do with the ball should it come their way. For Team B, I was constantly waiting for the batters to take their stance in the batter's box. They seldom swung at pitches even down the middle of the plate. And worst of all, their small catcher had trouble stopping anything the pitcher threw. He wasn't able to throw consistently within the strike zone, so Team A's batters made the best of the close bad pitches.

The game was played at Alliance's Earley's Hill #5 field, one of those open-sided fields where errant throws wind up to the lawn-chaired spectators or, once they moved out of the way, could roll forever in dead territory. By the third inning, I lost count of how many times I had been hit by a passed ball or wild pitch (not that I actually do count such things during a game). I couldn't say anything because no one else on Team B appeared willing to stand behind home plate to catch. The score had to be so lopsided I really didn't want to know until the fifth inning, so I could use the Mercy Rule and end the game.

Life Behind The Mask

In the fourth inning, three or four pitches in a row got by the catcher but surely found their way to my shins or face mask or arms. I tried to hide down behind my balloon chest protector and shin guards while seeing any pitch over the plate. Still I got hit.

Finally, it happened. A pitch came in about chest high on the batter, right down the heart of the plate. I felt sure the batter would launch it into orbit. But he never swung. The catcher knew the batter would take care of the ball, he never moved his glove to stop it. The next thing on its trajectory was the front of my face mask. It had to be the hardest pitch the young man had thrown all day because it knocked me back a couple of steps from my crouched position. The backstop at this field was twelve feet behind home plate, but still close enough. I backed right into it and fell on the seat of my pants. That was the last straw. I was in pain, and now I was embarrassed. My mask was askew on my face. I took it off with my right hand as I tried to stand up. Falling down again, I threw the mask to the other side of the backstop in anger. Undoubtedly the players in the home plate area were startled by my actions.

I stood up. Before I could take two steps, my father was standing in front of me. Apparently Buck had been watching the game. He stepped forward to stop me from doing something I really didn't mean to do – frighten this young pitcher.

"What are you doing?" he asked. He was calm and projected the control over me that I should have hadmyself.

I pointed out the pitcher and loudly said, "I'm taking a beating back here tonight." Fear crept over the boy's face and maybe a tear or two.

"And that's his fault how?" Buck asked. "You need to get out of the way of his pitches."

"Well," I tried to counter, "the catcher needs to stop a few of those balls from hitting me," I was trying to put the blame on anyone but myself.

"You're twenty-one-years-old, he's only eight. Don't you think you can move a little faster than him?"

I couldn't argue with the logic. "Yes, sir," I told him in a sheepish tone.

"Then apologize to these people and let's finish this game."

He handed me my face mask and stepped back to let me continue.

I told the catcher I was sorry for making him work so hard and shouted out to the pitcher something like "C'mon now, let's see a few more pitches like that one. Right in the strike zone." He smiled as I turned back to face the spectators behind the backstop. "Sorry, folks. Lost my head."

I put the face mask back on as Buck gave me a swat on the seat of my pants and stepped off the field.

When I got home after that game, he sat me down at the kitchen table. "Well, what did you learn tonight?"

I swallowed hard. "I learned I probably won't be doing any more umpiring."

"Only if that's what you want." He'd already spoken with the league's Umpire-In-Chief to explain the situation. "But did you learn anything else?"

"Yes, sir," I said, "I learned I've got to get out of the way more often. And when I don't, it's my own fault."

It was a positive lesson again. That was Buck's whole approach to things. I can't necessarily say it was fun, but obviously I went back the next day. And for many days thereafter.

* * *

During the other case, I didn't have Buck at the field. It was several years later and I'd been umpiring for about a decade, maybe a little more. It was in the eleven-and-twelve-year-old bracket at Earley's Hill #3 so the play was a degree better than the previous youngsters and these runners could lead off and steal the bases. This one pitcher could throw heat and he could place his pitches. He wasn't Johnny Holly, but he certainly wasn't all over the backstop. I could see this catcher was accustomed to being behind the plate for this young man because he kept a moist sponge in the glove to absorb the impact of the fastball. I knew this because I'd have to change out the ball at least once an inning in order to keep a dry one in the game. This pitcher was maybe twelve years old and really had command of his pitches. In truth he should have moved up to the next division because of his ability but by age he played in "G" League.

Very few balls were getting by the catcher but even more were meeting the bats for hits. The defensive effort kept them in the game because on offense, his teammates were not giving him much run support. The score may have been a five-to-five tie for all I knew. As I said before, I really don't concern myself with the score until we reach the fifth inning.

The manager for the opposing team, Dave, was a friend of mine with whom I had worked at a gas station in town right after college. He gave me a playful hard time with some calls. If we didn't have our good-natured history, I might have taken offense to some of his comments about my ability to see a white covered sphere that was no more than 9 1/4 inches in circumference. I'd joke with him being too close to his runner from the third base coach's box and, because he was so young, I was having trouble telling who was the runner and who was the coach. In retort, he'd offer me a chair to sit on between innings because I was *so* much older than he. It was an exceptionally enjoyable evening of play and I had no idea what to expect.

In this game, obviously I should have been concerning myself with something other than the score in the fifth inning. It was the top of the fifth and this pitcher was still on the mound and still throwing with controlled heat (no pitch-count limits at this time).

After one out, with a runner on second, Dave's clean-up batter stepped up to the plate. He'd made good contact on previous at-bats and this pitcher wanted to send a message with a strikeout.

The first pitch was a fast curve starting inside and then cut to the center of the plate as the batter stepped back out of its way. "Strike one," I declared. The next pitch was another curve ball but broke too soon and wound up outside the strike zone. "One ball, one strike," I announced to the players and spectators. A change-up the batter did not offer at brought the count to 2 and 1.

It was the next pitch that I will never forget; it was straight down the heart of the plate with a fastball and right at the batter's letters for a high strike. But I never got to call it. The catcher never raised his glove to stop it and the batter's swing would have been way under the ball. It was coming right at my face and I couldn't move out of the way in case it would break outside the strike zone. I had to watch it. I had to keep my eye on the ball to watch it cross the plate and make the call.

Crouched behind the catcher with my big black outside balloon chest protector firmly in my left hand, I stood there to adjudicate the pitch. At the last second, like a game of chicken on the highway, I flinched and turned my head to the left. I've told catchers hundreds of times not to turn their heads. "That's why we have all this equipment on in front of us—to stop the ball from hurting us when we get hit."

But I didn't listen to my own advice. I didn't duck out of the way, I didn't tilt my head to the side. Instead I just turned my head to the left and exposed the right side of my head to this fastball coming right at me. It struck me square on the point of my jawbone.

I rocked back to the seat of my pants and then onto my back. My knees were still tucked up underneath me in the crouched position. I probably looked like a turtle turned over on his back. Or so they told me because I was out cold. This pitch knocked me out.

It hit right on the right spot on my jawbone and rattled my head . . . to knock me out. The managers say I was only out a split second and I'll take their word for it. When I was able to focus my eyes, still looking through the bars of my facemask, Dave was kneeling over me. "You okay, Michael?" he asked, forgetting protocol about calling an umpire 'Blue' during a game.

I straightened out my legs and said I was fine. I tried to get up but between my rubbery legs and Dave's hands on my shoulders holding me down, my first attempt was unsuccessful.

"Just hold on, Blue," the other manager was saying. "We need to make sure you're okay."

I heard the catcher asking, "What was that pitch? Was it a strike?"

"Oh, yeah, that was a strike," I answered jokingly. "Struck me right on my jaw." Everybody laughed, glad to see that I was able to joke about the situation.

Dave helped me to stand up on one knee but would not let me go enough to stand up entirely. "Michael," he asked very seriously, "where are we?"

"Earley's Hill #3," I told him. I was right and I knew it.

"And who's playing?"

"Ah, Dave, you know I never deal with details like that." I was being totally honest. But then I told him who his team was. "And I'm really not sure who these guys are. But I know that pitcher has a … a heck of an arm." I pushed my way to stand up as I noticed the pitcher was also in the circle around me. I reached over to rub his head. "That's quite a fastball," I told him loud enough for everybody to hear and then leaned over to speak softly to him, "but can we tone it down to about ninety miles an hour, please?"

He laughed and said he'd try. The circle broke up as Dave handed me my mask he apparently removed from my face. "Are you sure you can finish the game, Blue?" he asked, back in protocol.

I put my hand on his shoulder and answered seriously, "If I can't, you'll be the first to know. Okay?"

He agreed and we finished the game. I suppose I should have gone to the emergency room to get checked out, but I went home and took a nice warm shower and then, at almost nine o'clock at night, ate supper.

But I learned not to turn my head. And I went back the next night for another game. And, boy, did I have fun?

* * *

Somewhere on some sandlot many, many years ago Larry, Curly, and Moe must have played baseball because there are so many plays and situations you could just see those three knuckleheads doing.

The game was a thirteen-and fourteen-year-old division contest in the afternoon. With runners on first and third and I believe two outs, I was in the field of a two-man umpiring crew in the inside "C" position. The batter popped a towering fly ball in between the right and center fielders.

The right fielder was an active player who would try to catch anything not hit in the infield, whether he should or not. In this case, the center fielder was the better of the two players, in a better angle on the ball. The right fielder started moving to his right, wildly waving his arms and shouting, "I've got it! I've got it!" I moved out so I could see the catch but still keep an eye on the runners, not to be in their way when I returned to the infield. As I set myself, I wondered why the runners weren't moving off the bases if there were in fact two outs.

Being the field umpire, I was not supposed to have an indicator so I was beginning to question myself as to how many outs had already been recorded this half-inning. It was too late to ask now so I knew I'd have to just go with the play and presume there were less than two outs.

As the ball started coming down, the right fielder was

still shouting, "I've got it! I've got it!" but his arm movements weren't as big as they were before because the flight of the ball had come right in front of the sun.

Suddenly I heard the center fielder chime in, "No, you don't!"

More determined than ever, the right fielder again began a chorus of "I've got it! I've got it!" while trying to shade his eyes with his gloved hand and find the ball in the sun.

The center fielder continued to express, "No, you don't!" but to no avail. It was very comedic to hear these two young teenagers exchanging "I've got it! I've got it!" and "No, you don't!"

From my perspective with the sun behind me, I stole a quick look up to see that the ball was going to drop about ten feet to the left of where the shouting right fielder stood. The center fielder, who had a little bit different angle on the ball, knew what he was saying. Apparently the coach at third base could see this, too, because he shouted to his players on base. "Run! Run! He's gonna drop it! He's gonna drop it! Run!"

Right in the middle of an "I've got it!" the fielder realized he couldn't pick the ball out in the sun-filled sky. Suddenly he changed to, "No, I don't! I can't see it!" At that point the ball was too close to the ground for the center fielder to get around behind his teammate and be in any position to make a catch. The ball fell safely to the ground.

Now the runner originally on first was forced to advance to second base as the batter/runner now stood on first base. The center fielder quickly pounced on the spheroid and fired a shot in to second base but the throw pulled the shortstop off the base and the runner slid safely. By this point the runner from third had scored.

Can you imagine what happened next? Nope, whatever you thought, that wasn't it. The defensive coach, a hefty man of maybe five foot nine inches tall but well over 300 pounds, charged out of the third base dugout to confront not the umpire but the offensive coach at third base, a six-foot-something tall, lean gentleman who appeared he wouldn't hurt a fly. But this wasn't a fly confronting him on the field in front of all these spectators. "You made him drop that ball!" he repeatedly shouted in the man's face, complete with finger pointing.

After a quick look to make sure all of the runners would stay where they were, my partner and I both called "Time!" simultaneously and each broke into a run towards third base. We were both of the mind we had to get these two adults separated before any punches were thrown. Like hockey officials, once punches are being thrown between adults, I am not about to put myself in the middle of that melee.

The defensive coach was continuing with his shouting: "You caused my boy to drop that ball!" When he saw both umpires approaching on a dead run, he turned his attention to us. "You heard what he said. He distracted my boy from catching that ball!"

Suddenly the words were adding up. Now it all made sense. The reason the right fielder was basically running the field was being the coach's son. To this father, his boy could do no wrong. And, if he did, there would always be somebody else to blame for it. My partner took up the peacekeeper role.

"Coach, he was shouting instructions to his players. He's allowed to do that, you know. He wasn't shouting at your fielder."

"But my boy could hear him. That's unsportsmanlike conduct. That batter should be out." He was pointing at the batter/runner standing on first base. Unfortunately my partner took a second to try to get his head wrapped around that logic. The coach was attempting to apply a football penalty to a baseball situation. The coach took his hesitation as an indication the umpire might be sympathetic to his position. "He's out, right? That batter should be out!"

Finally, the home plate umpire shook his head. "Nope. Don't see it that way. All hands are safe," he said complete with the big arm motion to indicate safe. He turned to head back to home plate and said, "Let's get back to the game, gentlemen." I took his lead and turned to head back to the "C" position with runners on first and second.

The defensive coach, though, wasn't quite finished and started to follow my partner to say something further. Without turning around, the umpire said loudly, "To the bench or to the parking lot, Coach. I don't care which. But don't make me decide for you."

The point was taken and the game resumed. I did my best not to chuckle for the rest of the inning at the objection and at my partner's interesting way of handling the coach. I'd have to remember that if I ever had that situation.

Rules for Every Umpire to Live By

Within the rulebook is a section devoted entirely to the adjudicators of the regulations. It takes up just over three pages of text and then has "friendly advice" for the men in blue. It covers such things as not trying to get friendly with the players because somewhere during a game you will make a call that could upset them or a call in their favor that could encourage the wrath of personnel from an opposing team.

The umpires are urged to carry a rulebook with them and to consult it when they might not understand the application in a particular situation. I would think the last thing an umpire should do is pull out a rulebook to look for an interpretation of a rule on the field. If you don't know that rulebook and how to apply it to all matter of knotty problems at a moment's notice, maybe you ought not to be on the field. If you do blow a call and, with the assistance of your other umpires, can correct it at that time, do not hesitate to ask for a conference. But *never, never, never* admit to anyone after a game you blew a call and didn't take steps to correct it at the time. Doing such, Tim McClelland (a major league umpire for nearly 30 years), only holds a spotlight up on all umpires and encourages the public to second-guess every call made on the field. I've heard many commentators suggest after an umpire has made one bad call, he attempts to even it up by making a second call favorable to the aggrieved team. Nothing could be further from the truth, and if any umpire actually does such, he should be removed from umpiring. That's just my opinion, mind you, but I am not afraid to express it.

It would be a fair statement to say most managers, and possibly a few umpires, do not realize those suggestions are printed within the official rulebook. Several years ago in the Ohio Hot Stove Baseball League, it was suggested that the men and women who serve as umpires should dress the part and look uniform while conducting a contest. The lead was taken from the Major League Umpires at the time who wore light gray slacks with a black belt, black shoes with no insignia, and generally light blue dress shirts with short sleeves. It was explained by the local chapter's Umpire-In-Chief, who himself was a former minor league umpire, that even if you got a call wrong, if you looked like a professional umpire you had a better chance of convincing the spectators and perhaps more importantly the managers that you knew what you were doing and were right. And, to a degree, it works. Not that I have ever made a mistake or a wrong call while umpiring a game … except for probably one or two each and every game. The important thing to remember when you know you have blown a call and it's too late to correct it is not try to even things up with another call. The bad call you made is over and done with; now just work your hardest to get all the other ones correct. If that means taking an extra second or two before indicating that safe or out or the ball or strike, then take those few extra seconds. It's more important to be right than to be quick. There is no race to make the correct call in this sport. Admittedly, I have had coaches who will make a call before the umpire that would encourage spectators or opposing managers to argue that the umpire was allowing the coach to make the calls for him. So it's a fine line to walk but not one that the umpires are unaccustomed to doing. Be sure and convincing with every call. Umpiring is not a piecework job. The quality end product is much more important.

As a one-man crew, it is far too easy to be out of position on a play. The key is to hustle to be as close to the proper position as you can and then stop and get set before the play occurs to make that call. The coaches encourage the players to hustle out to their positions between innings and the umpire needs to hustle to be in position for every call. An umpire should never be making a call while still running towards the play. Why? Because, in moving at any speed, your head could be bobbing up and down with each step and therefore you'd have to be resetting your vision at the play with each running step you are taking. It is especially true when you are taking those last few steps to stop and get set for the play. If you are doing this when the play is taking place, it leaves too much room for error. But, if you are stopped and set for the call, you have a better chance of seeing the play clearly and correctly, making the 100% correct call, and being able to convince everyone in the park it was right. Remember, get as close to the play as you possibly can to still see everything and then get set up make the correct call.

*   *   *

There are about 206 bones in the human body. Some points of high school biology you just never forget no matter how useless the information may seem at the time. These I can recall at a moment's notice, but why then do I always have to look up my neighbor's telephone number?

I mention this trivial little fact about the human body because so far in my lifetime I have broken only five or six bones and most have been at the baseball field. I broke two bones in my right forearm when I was maybe eight years old and was the batboy for my brother's team. The season was maybe two weeks old and it was very early summer. The incident actually happened before the game started.

There was a big A-frame metal chain swing set near the baseball field and I was just wasting time before the game. I was swinging very high when my mother called me to come to the field as the game was starting. To this day I remember my response. "One more swing," I said. And when I reached the top of the back swing, I prepared for a grand gymnastic dismount.   As I moved forward past the bottom of the swing, I let go of the metal chains to jump off the seat. Except my left hand didn't let go at the same time as my right and I fell off crooked. To break my fall, I extended my arms. My intent was to land on my hands, roll into a summersault and come up on my feet and wait for the judges' scores. That was what went through my eight-year-old mind in those few seconds in flight. I mean, how hard could it be? I had seen the gymnasts do it on TV dozens of times. However, that wasn't how it happened.

With most of my weight on my right side when I landed, the two bones in the right forearm fractured on impact and I crumpled to the ground in sudden pain.

Because we only had one car in the family, and because Dad and my brother had to stay at the field for their game, I didn't go to the emergency room until after the game was over. The bones were set and the arm put in a plaster cast for six-to eight-weeks. And I learned not to jump off the swings again, at least until I was much older.

I never said all of these stories were going to be extremely exciting but it sets up the next tale.

More recently, I was umpiring behind the plate of a twelve-and-under game, I decided to wear my field shoes for the game because the fields at this park were soft and I felt I needed to be able to dig in to get in a good position in the slot.

Like most umpires, I have two different types of shoes to use for umpiring. The field shoes are rubber spikes for moving quickly around the infield to get in proper position for the calls on the bases. The shoes I wear when behind the plate are actually steel-toed work shoes designed to give protection to the toes from foul balls. In hindsight I should have been wearing those shoes that evening.

It was about the fourth inning of the game and I was feeling very comfortable behind the plate. I was able to move about well and not get bogged down in the loose soil. Then, of course, it happened. The batter swung up on top of a waist-high pitch and fouled it downwards, right back toward the catcher. Except it went to his left side where I was set up in the slot. There's probably some law of physics that says when the bat hits the ball, its speed increases because of the momentum of the swing. The spheroid was a direct hit on the grand toe of my unprotected left foot. I knew immediately upon impact it was broken.

Being a foul ball, of course, the ball was dead and further action could not take place. Before the catcher had a chance to get up from his squat position to retrieve the ball, which doubtless bounced off the side toward the backstop, I heavily placed my right hand on his shoulder for support and told him, "Stay down there a minute, will you?" He wasn't exactly sure why but he did as I asked.

That little action did not escape the notice of one of the bench coaches. "You okay, Blue?" he asked from the dugout.

"Not this time," was my honest reply. I was able to shift my weight over to my uninjured right foot and allow the catcher to go recover the ball. I attempted to wiggle the toes of my left foot but discovered that only caused more pain. The coach came out to me. In fact, I believe members of both teams' coaching staffs came out to home plate.

The question was asked again, "You okay, Blue?" by one of the gentlemen.

"I think I broke my toe." I seriously replied. I think initially they thought I was joking but then accepted that I was being completely honest. I have been injured on the ball field before but seldom will admit to it then, probably in order not to give the coaches and spectators ammunition against me later in the game. The standard joke is, after a foul ball has bounced off my chest protector or shoulder where there is no chest protector, after I have called a 'foul' ball, someone will ask, "Was that foul or 'ow'?"

One of the coaches told a player to go get some ice for my foot. "No need, coach," I said. "To put ice on the foot, I'd have to take my shoe off. If I take my shoe off, my foot would swell up so much I'd never get the shoe back on to finish the game."

"That, and we'd all pass out," one of the coaches offered in an attempt at some humor, since apparently I wasn't offering any.

"Blue, finishing the game is irrelevant if you've got a broken foot," another coach offered. At this time I had backed up to the backstop and was leaning against it to get the weight and pressure off my foot.

"It's not the foot, it's just the big toe. And if I leave now and go to the emergency room, all they can do is take X-rays and tell me it's broken." I finally suggested. "I mean, it's not like they can put a cast on it.

"It's a big toe. The best they could do is tape it to the next toe and tell me to stay off it for a couple of days."

"Yeah, and give you some whopping painkillers," suggested one of the younger coaches. It brought some chuckles again but I had one goal in mind and that was to finish this game, as I was the only umpire for this field. I'd worry about the toe later.

Fortunately no more foul balls went off the foot the remainder of the night and, yes, I did finish the game although I couldn't tell you who won or by what margin. Then I went straight home and took some ibuprofen, put an ice bag over the toe and did not go to the emergency room. The next day at work I was in considerable pain but knew there was little that could be done other than more ibuprofen, which I took.

The following night I had another game. Dressing at home before driving to the field, I discovered that the toe was still painful and somewhat swollen such that I could not put my steel-toed shoe on and would have to wear the field shoes again for this game behind the plate. Did I ever consider calling off for the night? The thought never entered my mind. Until about the fourth inning when another foul ball found its way to the same grand toe once again.

Yes, I finished that game, too. Yes, I took some more

ibuprofen, iced the foot down again at home. And, yes, I went to work, the next day being a Friday. But while at work, I called for a doctor's appointment thinking that might be a quicker route than waiting for three or more hours in an emergency room. My doctor was able to get me in that afternoon and had X-rays taken at the medical center there. Guess what? The left grand toe was broken but there was nothing they could do about it.

I was given a seven-day supply of painkiller samples (I appreciate doctors who provide sample medicines I don't have to pay for), a prescription for antibiotics and told to stay off the foot for a couple of days. I was also told the toenail had been dislodged from the toe, probably from the second hit, and I would lose it but it would eventually grow back.

I still walk with a slight limp as the toe obviously did not heal 100% the way it had been but I can still walk and, when I get on the field, the adrenaline gets rushing and I very seldom feel any pain (at least not that I would admit to). However, once the game is over and I am in my car driving home I begin to feel some, but I know I've done a good job for the players that evening. And, oh yes, regardless of the field conditions, when I'm working behind the plate now, I am wearing the steel-toed shoes. Nothing like closing the barn door after the horse has gotten out, but it won't happen again (I hope).

The moral of these stories: if you have a severe injury at the field, go to the emergency room or your doctor as soon as possible to get a diagnosis and treatment and then follow the doctor's orders. What's that you say? That's not what I did? And your point?

Do as I say, not as I do. I would never let a player (or a coach) with an obvious broken bone or severe injury continue to stay at the field. I would insist that medical attention be sought immediately even if I had to call for the ambulance myself. Most leagues have a rule that a player or coach or even an official cannot go on the field with an open wound. Two reasons for that are to prevent any foreign bodies (dirt, grass, etc.) from infecting the wound and as a reaction years ago to the spread of AIDS before too much was known about it.

The players have their entire lives before them and shouldn't ignore an injury that could jeopardize their health. With the adult coaches, that is someone's parent and they have responsibilities larger than just that game to those individuals. And, there would be other parents able to step up and finish their duties at the field for that evening.

But the umpire, especially when he's the only umpire at the field, has no one else to complete the task for him. Yes, I had obligations away from the field with family and work but, like many of the people who are umpires, I have this Superman complex and feel I am irreplaceable to the game. But believe me, if an injury were severe, I would be the first to call for the ambulance and take myself out of the game. But, as long as it doesn't interfere with my ability to make fair and accurate calls, in order to finish the game, I'll stay. With a broken toe already well supported inside the shoe as this was, or an extreme foul ball shot to the shoulder, the arm, the leg, or somewhere else, as some football player said "Rub some dirt on it."

*   *   *

Over the course of over forty years of umpiring, I went from an athletic teenager just starting out in the business to a middle-aged man then an active grandfather. And through the years my physique has changed considerably. Therefore my umpiring clothes changed as well. For a considerable amount of time in Ohio I could obtain the gray slacks from a used work clothes store in town in the various sizes as the need arose at very economical prices.

Unfortunately, at times I might take a pair of slacks out of the closet that were the wrong size. As home plate umpire with the youngest of players, sometimes their strike zones can be very small and very low to the ground requiring a much lower stance. I like to have my head in the slot, of course, between the catcher and the batter at about the top of the strike zone (said to be a midway point between the collar of the shirt and top of the waist). I've never been a member of a gym or athletic club and don't have a regular workout routine because, at least during baseball season, I get my exercises in with anywhere from 150 to 200 deep knee bends or more and untold distances of short burst running each night behind the plate and especially on the field.

In those years, however, I have had two instances where the pants I wore would not allow me to get down in that deep knee bend. What does that mean? Yes, the back seam of the slacks ripped open. A pair I recently purchased at a clothing store where police officers obtain their uniforms fell victim to this condition at their first outing. I felt the custom alterations should be reliable. Well, apparently the seamstress didn't get the message to allow enough room for repeated squatting. On both occasions the back seam may have started as a slight separation of the threads but wound up being ripped open from belt loop on top to the bottom of the zipper underneath.

Fortunately, I carry a towel with me to the fields to wipe the perspiration from my face and arms so I was able to tuck the towel in the back waist of my slacks and let it hang much like a football center would have a towel for the quarterback to wipe his hands. After all, for the one year in junior high school I played organized football, my position was offensive center. And, yes, the pants went back to the seamstress for repairs right after they were laundered. My fear is that someone captured that embarrassing exposure and there is a videotape or at least a photograph of it out there on the Internet or worse yet somebody's video submission to a TV program. I don't think appearances like that would qualify me for a SAG card.

Life Behind The Mask

*   *   *

One winter I decided to do something about my weight. It had gotten to the point of stepping on the scales and going beyond what the scale would measure. I needed to shop at big and tall men's stores to get 54" waist slacks. That, of course, included two pair of umpiring slacks that I would have to launder frequently. So, during the holidays, perhaps the absolute worst time of the year to try it, I decided to knock off a few pounds. I had no specific goal in mind and happy to say, between November and February I dropped thirty-five pounds!

When I was called for the first game of the spring season in February, I pulled out my large-waisted umpiring slacks and found the 54" slacks to be extremely loose. But I wasn't yet down to the 50" size and certainly not the 48" ones. So I took a belt and cinched up the 54" slacks as tight as I could around my waist, folded in the pants where I could (by more than two inches!) and went to the ball field.

I needed to keep hiking up the pants because they were so loose. I got a few favorable comments from spectators who had seen me the previous year and wanted to know how I dropped so much weight, it was that evident. When I am umpiring a game, I feel the players are obviously there to have fun so why shouldn't I enjoy the game as well? Around the third inning of the game, I jokingly stepped into the left-handed batter's box while a new pitcher was throwing his warm-up tosses. "Come on," I encouraged him standing as if bat in hand, "let's see what you got."

The pitch was tight and about chest high. I jokingly leaned back away from the pitch and then challenged the pitcher, "Are you trying to hit me?" He shook his head that it was indeed his intent to dust me off (he was kidding around, right?). He chuckled as I stepped back in the box and this time put my mask on. "Okay, son," I said. "Bring it." And so he did.

The pitch buzzed by my head and went to the backstop

as the catcher could not get in front of it. In order to give him time to retrieve the ball and to give the pitcher a new ball as doubtlessly the previous one would be dirty, I took off the mask and began to charge the mound. It was a good show as the pitcher set himself for the confrontation. Except for one thing.

Remember those extremely loose slacks? With each step I took toward the mound, the slacks slipped lower from my waist. Before I got to the mound, the back of the slacks had slipped below my cheeks (yes, I was wearing gray sliding pants beneath) as I was holding on to the front with my free hand.

As I handed the pitcher a fresh ball from the bag on my hip, I proceeded to lift the pants back up where they should be and tucked in the shirt. Returning to the home plate area, I commented to the spectators behind the backstop, "That's what I get from losing thirty-five pounds in the off-season." There's another Internet opportunity I fear I may see someday. And, absolutely, both pairs of the umpiring pants went to the seamstress the next day to be taken in by more than two inches each.

But, you know what? That really felt good!

* * *

Soon after my older brother, Bob, and I began umpiring back in the mid-1970s, we had an opportunity to work a high school level game as a three-man crew with our father, Buck. He had home plate (and Umpire-In-Chief for our little crew), Bob took the first base/right field line position, and I was at third base/left field line. The game progressed smoothly. So much so that I could not have told you the amount of runs scored or which team, if either, were ahead.

With a runner on second and one out, the batter lifted a tall fly ball deep into left field. I shouted, "I've got the ball" as I headed out to judge the catch and whether the ball would be fair or foul. I knew this would leave Buck covering third base should the runner on second attempt to advance. With the balloon type outside chest protector firmly in his left hand, he advanced up the third base line to watch the potential catch and the runner tagging up at second. Bob was left on the right side of the field to monitor the batter/runner should the ball drop.

As the ball reached its zenith and began its descent, the left fielder took a position one step inside the foul line to catch it. As the wind carried the ball inward, he adjusted about a half of step further inside the field. Then another step back towards the left field position. As the ball fell closer to Earth, the unthinkable happened. This high school player stepped on his own foot and fell to the ground as the ball dropped not four feet away from him.

I automatically extended my arms outward to indicate no catch. "It's on the ground," I shouted and returned my eyes to the infield to see where the runners (and more importantly, my fellow umpires) were positioned.

With the ball on the ground, the runner from second shot off for third base where Buck waited to make a call. The alert center fielder, backing up the play, scooped up the spheroid and fired it into third base.

This runner showed no intention of stopping at third.

Before the ball was thrown in, he already rounded the bag, heading for home. Bob could see Buck would be out of position at home. He shouted, "I've got home," and broke for the plate.

That left the batter/runner now for me to cover. Still at first base, he chose that time to break for second. I ran top speed toward the infield to get closer to second while letting Buck know second was mine and I needed him to stay at third should the batter/runner have visions of a triple.

The throw came in to the cutoff man. He cranked up for a throw to home plate. When he saw any throw would be too late, he turned and fired to the second baseman covering the keystone sack.

I stood near the edge of the outfield grass when the play developed. The batter/runner slid into the bag. The ball arrived simultaneously. The fielder caught the ball and swept his hand down to make a tag on the sliding batter/runner.

The ball came out of his glove in the motion and rolled several feet away. The batter/runner saw this, made a hook slide on the bag to jump up and head for third where Buck waited.

The right fielder recovered the errant baseball and threw it to the waiting third baseman. The runner previously on second scored without a play so Bob took a look at the developing play and decided he needed to stay at home should the batter/runner do the impossible. Instead, though, he became caught in a run-down between second and third with Buck still holding on to his balloon chest protector covering third base and me at second.

After two or three throws back and forth, the batter/runner dove headfirst towards second base. He received a face full of leather glove before his hand touched the bag. My right arm pumped downward and quickly back up. "He's out!" (Sell that call!)

The play was done and the umpires were all out of their normal position but very much in proper positions. The players on the teams may be able to shout to one another about their good play and slap each other on the behind or the shoulders or give high-fives, but umpires – we don't do such things. At least not on the field. Our signal to each other is to close our hands into fists and tap our right hand over the left hand as if on a baseball bat. In umpires' hand signals it means good call or good positioning. As Buck, Bob, and I each returned to our proper positions, we displayed to the others a hand tap. Best play of the day, I'd have to say.

*   *   *

I am very dedicated to youth baseball organizations.

Truth be told, as a youngster I felt I was a pretty good player and had a future ahead of me in the sport. This, of course, is the dream of many a kid who plays ball. I have also been asked, with my devotion to the game, why I never pursued a career as an umpire. The honest answer is I was having too much fun as an umpire for the youth leagues. I didn't want to spoil it by making it a vocation as opposed to just an avocation.

When I started in this business, umpires received five dollars a game if they worked as a field umpire, seven dollars if they were the plate umpire of a two-man squad, and eight dollars if they did a game alone.

I don't know of too many chapters making a distinction in pay anymore but you could see the financial advantage for the chapter to have only one umpire. At that time, in the 1970s, that was a lot of money for a college student trying to get gas money to commute to school. Of course, remember gasoline was only 25.9 cents a gallon (oh, for those days again!) and the minimum wage was $1.60 an hour (I don't want to see those days again!), so eight bucks for maybe two hours' work was great money.

One summer I saved all of my umpiring money, around three hundred dollars. During the post–season tournament, when the host organization's volunteers would pass through the crowds with their donation buckets for the chapter, I put an envelope in the bucket with that money.

Oh, to have been a fly on the wall in that counting room when the league officials opened that envelope. I love this game.

When the elementary school two of my daughters attended held a fund-raising carnival at the end of the school year, complete with various games of skill, I volunteered to go up in the dunking tank. I mentioned this at a couple of games during the week before, and, to say the least, the response was surprisingly favorable. For some reason there were a large number of parents and managers wanting to take the opportunity of dunking an umpire. I attempted to point out that I was not doing this as an umpire but as a member of the parents' organization. Then someone came up with the dare. "I'll bet you wouldn't go up there in full umpire's gear."

Reminding them there was no betting in baseball, I asked what it would be worth to them if I would.

"You're serious?"

"I am if you are." Since I couldn't profit personally from this, a contribution to the youth baseball organization would be made if I went on the chair in full gear.

I was there for about an hour with shin guards, inside chest protector, hat, clothes and mask (I wouldn't wear the baseball shoes because they could get damaged from the water and would take forever to dry out – not to mention, being steel-toed, could make it difficult to climb out of the tank). I was probably dunked a half-dozen times. The line was constant and even included a few of the youngsters. Just for show, I taunted the throwers. "You can't hit the strike zone during a game. What makes you think you can hit this little bull's-eye target now?"

One coach, whom I had ejected the previous year. Must have spent twenty dollars trying to dunk me with no avail. "That explains a lot," I told him from the chair.

How much did I raise? I don't remember exactly but I was told it was the best hour of the carnival for the dunking tank. Can't imagine why. I had fun, the throwers had fun (some of them a little too much, perhaps) and the school's parents' organization made some money, as did the baseball league for my efforts. It was the talk of the fields for the remainder of the summer as people who didn't make it to that carnival wanted to know when I would be doing it again.

Several years ago I made a return visit to the tank for a Florida Little League chapter and even encouraged other umpires to do so. It was, as expected, a good time for the participants and profitable for the chapter.

*   *   *

When you are the only umpire on the field, there's no field umpire with whom to confer about a better angle on a call. There is no field umpire to ask, "Did he go?" when a batter takes a half swing and you're not sure if he broke his wrists or not. So you have to see it all. You have to know all the rules and how they apply to any situation during the course of a game. You can't determine before the game starts, "I won't call any infield flies tonight so I don't need to remind myself when it's in effect." As part of the umpires' signals to one another during the game, when the infield fly could be called, the home plate umpire will use one of three signals. Either he taps himself on top of his cap, he taps the front of his mask with the palm of his hand for no outs or with the index finger pointing up indicating one out, or he will pound a closed fist into his chest protector a few times to make the sound as well as the hand signal. Which signal an umpiring crew will use is decided before they ever take the field. But when you have a one-man crew, it's just as important to give yourself the signals for two reasons. The action is a physical reminder the call is in play. Secondly, so many managers who umpire know that signal and realize the umpire is aware of the situation.

A few years ago I was working a game in Akron, with a youth umpire (a fourteen-year-old boy who was learning the game) and the Infield Fly Rule came into play. I called time and motioned for him to meet me halfway between home plate and the pitcher's mound for he was positioned on the infield grass between the mound and second base.

"Anything I need to know about this situation?" I tested him.

"Why? What's the matter?" he asked, afraid he had done something wrong.

"Nothing's the matter but we have two runners on base."

"So I need to be behind the pitcher, right?"

"Yes, you were in position," I assured him. "But what else is going on?" I pointed to the location of the two runners and then held my indicator out for him to see. It showed no outs.

Although a field umpire should not carry an indicator, I felt it might help him be aware of the game situations so he had one. He checked his indicator and discovered it did not agree with mine (which is why a field umpire should not be carrying an indicator). While clicking it to match mine, he looked at me and asked, "How did you know I had one out on my indicator?"

I suppressed a chuckle as I answered my paranoid partner, "I didn't. But there's something else I do know about two runners on and no outs." He didn't bite so I told him. "Infield Fly Rule is in effect. Now, you know what that is?"

"Oh, yeah," he answered. "With runners on first and second and one or no outs, if the batter hits a fly ball, he's out and the runners advance one base."

I dropped my head. Not even close. I wasn't about to pull out my rulebook here in the middle of the game to show this young man so I tried to explain to him. "No," I said. "With runners on first and second or first, second and third with a force-out possible but less than two outs, if the batter hits a fly ball that can be caught by an infielder, the batter is automatically out but the runners have to wait for the ball to be touched by a fielder before they can leave their bag."

"If the infielder drops the ball, the batter can still run, right?" he asked.

"No, he's out even if the fielder misses the catch." I explained. This was taking too much time and I decided I'd explain the rest to him either between innings or after the game. Besides, the opportunity of an infield fly may occur several times during a game but the actual event occurs less than one time per game so the chances that it would be applied here were slim.

Back in our positions, I tapped my hand on top of my head to signal Infield Fly Rule potential, should the coaches not be aware, then called "Play ball!" The first pitch was outside the strike zone for ball one. The second pitch made it ball two. The third pitch, however, was lifted high into the air and heading for shallow right field.

As I set myself outside the third base line to watch the runners tag up. As the presumed catch was being made, my worst nightmare occurred. "Infield fly!" my young field umpire was yelling from his position behind the pitcher. He then turned and pointed to the batter as he was running down towards first base, "You're out!"

I had to cover up quickly. "No outs. No one is out!" I yelled. "Ball is alive and in play!" Just then the right fielder caught the ball. Now I had to make that call and make it with as much intensity as I could. I raised my right hand into the air with a clenched fist, pointed to the batter and shouted, "Right fielder caught the ball. *Now* the batter is out!"

Because of the confusion, no runners tried to advance as the right fielder threw the ball into the second baseman. As soon as the ball got back to the pitcher (and maybe even a second or two before), I called time and ran out to meet the field umpire. When I got to him, I put my arm around his shoulder and started walking towards the area between the second baseman and the right fielder as I talked. "That was *not* an infield fly. The right fielder had to back up to catch the ball." I explained,

"But there were runners on first and second," he countered.

"Yes, but the ball must be able to be caught by an *in*fielder," I repeated myself from before. "That's why we call it an 'infield fly.' It prevents a cheap double play if the fielder drops the ball."

"But he caught it," the field umpire said while pointing

to the right fielder.

I reached up and pulled his arm back down. "But he wasn't in the infield." I could see there wasn't enough time to explain this on the field. I assured him I would explain it in detail after the game.

Besides, at this point, the defensive team manager came out toward where we were standing. "What gives?" he asked. "Is the batter out or not?"

I physically held the young umpire from turning around to direct his comments to the manager. Instead, I turned my head over my shoulder to tell him, "Coach, give us a minute, please. This is a youth umpire. The batter is out and the ball is now dead." I had to figure how to get out of this situation. "I'll be with you in a minute. Okay, Coach?"

He accepted it and went back to the infield. (He actually was talking with his pitcher when I got back to him which should have been counted as a trip to the mound but I let it slide … this time.)

Following the conclusion of the game I sat down with the youth umpire to explain the details of the infield fly. I did my best and hoped this young man understood it was a case of runners on first and second or first, second, and third with less than two outs but the pop-up or fly ball must be able to be caught by an infielder with normal effort.

The infielder does not have to be in the infield at the time of the catch for it to still be an infield fly. I can't tell you how many managers have told me, "But he was out in the outfield when he made the catch" and I've had to explain the portion about "with normal effort" isn't dictated by the outfield grass. I also had one instance where the pop-up behind the second baseman was actually caught by the right fielder charging in to take control of the situation but it was still an infield fly because the second baseman *could* have caught the ball with normal effort but was called off by the right fielder.

The call comes in handy but you have to know how *and*

when to apply it.

*   *   *

Years ago as a younger umpire, I had a problem occasionally making my calls too quick. As the home plate umpire, my right hand would be coming up for a strike call before the ball even crossed the plate. As the field umpire, I would be calling a runner out at first before the fielder caught the ball because the throw was so far ahead of the runner, there was no doubt of the expected result. And there were times where the call, if completed, would have been wrong as either the batter may actually have hit the ball or the first baseman failed to catch or at least cleanly contain the ball before the runner reached the bag.

I was told many times by other umpires, and even informed spectators, I needed to slow down my calls and not try to anticipate, especially with the younger players. It was my brother, Bob, who finally put it in terms that made complete sense. "When you're watching a major league game on TV," he said, "do you see the umpire make the call at first base?"

Of course you do.

"So the call comes after the play. After all the action has taken place, then you see the umpire make the call."

Obviously he was correct, but his explanation made all the difference.

"When the batter hits the ball, the director in the production truck shifts to the camera of the fielder picking up the ball and then throwing to first base where the next camera focuses on the first baseman as he is seen receiving the throw before the batter/runner crosses the base. Finally the camera view shifts to the umpire making the call.

"Wait for the camera," my brother explained to me. "Right then, for that time of the game, all eyes are on you to see what your decision is. If you hurry your call, not only is there a chance the call will be wrong, there's also a chance not everybody will see you make the call. And

174

that's a bad thing. Wait for the camera." Pausing a few seconds before giving that 'out' signal to be sure everyone is watching you.

"But don't wait too long or they may think you're having trouble with the call," he added. "Keep your focus on the play, don't turn your head unless it's to follow the path of the ball that got away from the fielder." And, when you make that call, do it standing up so everybody can see you and the call clearly.

"Wait for the camera and make the call sure and tall." Very good advice to any young umpire and even the veterans.

* * *

As the field umpire, I am constantly relocating myself on the field in relationship to the runners on base. With no runners on base, the standard "A" position is behind first base on the right field foul line.

With the runner on first, the best location in the youth game is behind the pitcher on the infield grass between first and second known as the "B" position. If the umpire positions himself on the infield grass, he must be mindful of the location of the second baseman and stay out of his line of vision of the batter and home plate. I try to stay in a crouched position to keep myself low to the fielders' lines of vision. More frequently, though, on the smaller fields I am on the outfield grass in a comparable position.

The key is always to be ahead of the runner on base and be able to see any potential play develop in front of my location while still being able to clearly see a pick-off play at the base where the runner is located.

The downside of moving around the field is you also have to be mindful of where the batter may hit the ball and to stay out of the way of an infielder that would be trying to field such a batted ball.

In a thirteen-and fourteen-year-old game with ninety foot base paths, a runner on second and one out. As the field umpire I positioned myself on the infield grass behind the pitcher, a step or two to the third base side and about halfway between the pitcher's mound and second base, in the "C" position. At this bracket of play, the runners could lead off and the pitcher would throw from a set position with pick-off plays possible. So I had to stay out of the way of any potential throw to second base to pick off the runner in his lead-off.

As the pitcher began his pitch to the batter, the runner on second headed for third base. I was positioned facing towards third to be able to see any play develop in front of me. As the runner left second base, I took two or three steps toward third base to be closer to the potential play. My focus was fixed on the runner and the crack of the bat didn't register with me until I felt the ball hit my right instep and ricochet toward the pitcher. Reflectively I raised both of my hands to the air. I looked around at the fielders and realized that no one had an opportunity to field the ball before it struck my foot. The umpire in chief and I both made the call at about the same time: "Dead ball!"

The third base coach was livid when I explained that the runner had to return to second base. "But he had third base made. There wasn't even going to be a play made on him." His objections were sound and made perfectly logical sense. But they ran contrary to the rule because the runner was not forced to advance to third. I also knew that I had, literally, really stepped into this one.

There are times when the expression "the umpire is part of the field" is correct. For example, if the field umpire in position behind the infielders on the smaller fields is struck by a ball that has already gone past a fielder (other than the pitcher) or strikes him after first being touched by a fielder then the contact with the umpire is incidental and play continues as if the contact never occurred. The only exception to that would be if the ball becomes lodged in the umpire's clothing or paraphernalia. Let's examine just such a play.

*   *   *

As home plate umpire, I would have extra balls for the game. For a number of years I would keep the extra balls in my right front pants pocket until I was able to have a black ball bag made to attach to my belt. This bag, as previously described, was made with a dark blue towel sewn inside the bag in order to wipe off the ball if it became wet or had mud attached. The bag was actually big enough to hold four balls being two rows of two balls each. The bag was very soft and pliable so I could feel how many balls were within just by touch.

The eleven-year-old batter had been fighting off the pitcher's 3–2 count with foul ball after foul ball. He must have successfully extended his at-bat by four pitches or more with foul balls. The pitcher tried fastball, change-up, and a ball right on the outside corner of the plate and each had been deflected into foul territory and then returned to the field of play for extended use. Finally, a fastball snuck past the swinging bat for strike three but the catcher did not stop the ball. In fact, it struck him on the right shoulder and deflected up to my mask. From there neither he nor I were sure where the ball went but the batter started to head for the bench. Since he didn't see the ball on the ground, he figured the catcher had it in his mitt. But he did not. This catcher looked around the ground in his immediate area as I straightened up from my crouched position behind him to get out of his way. He couldn't find the ball and neither could I.

I took off my mask and backed away from the catcher, heading backwards toward the third base side of the backstop figuring that since it bounced off my face mask, it must have been on the first base side of the area, maybe near the backstop in some weeds that the Parks and Recreation Department had not trimmed before the game. But it was not there either. By this time the batter had gone

177

back to his bench area and dropped his helmet and bat, resigned he had made the second out.

As I continued to back up from the catcher's search, I reached down and felt the ball bag. I could tell I had one too many balls in there. I raised my hands and shouted, "Time. Dead ball." All eyes were seemingly on me as I reached into my ball bag and pull out the lost ball.

"How did that get in there?" asked the catcher.

"Bounced off my face mask and into the bag, I would have to guess." I answered honestly. Then I turned to the offensive team bench. "Unfortunately the batter is out because he didn't run to first base."

"What do you mean?" asked the manager who had been coaching at third base. "The catcher caught the ball for strike three."

"No, I didn't," offered the young man. "It got away from me and apparently bounced into Blue's bag here." He took the ball from my hand and threw it out to his pitcher.

I walked over toward the manager to explain the rule to him as I knew it.

"Then he gets first base, right?"

"Well, he would if he had tried for it. But instead he went back to the bench thus abandoning any effort to advance to first base." I explained. "It's in the six hundreds, if he leaves the base path and heads for the dugout, once there, it's determined he's abandoned the effort to advance and is out."

So it's all the more important whenever the batter hits the ball, he should run to first base until the umpire calls it foul. And if the umpire calls "Strike three," in those leagues where it is appropriate, he should still run to first base. With first base open and less than two outs, the batter should always run out a presumed dropped third strike. The worst that could happen? He gets a little extra exercise. The best thing could be he'd be on first base and not out. The umpire should never indicate 'Strike Three. Batter is out" unless first base is occupied with less than two outs or he is 100% certain the catcher caught the ball cleanly.

The other side of running out that dropped third strike is the catcher may doubt if he cleanly caught the ball and throw to first to complete the out. With other runners on base, this may give them the opportunity to advance and even score. Although it would be a judgment call, the batter running to first base should not be viewed as attempting to confuse the defensive team players by his actions or making a travesty of the game if there is a genuine possibility that the catcher did not catch or cleanly possess the baseball on a third strike to the batter.

The Scorebook Is Very Important

In youth baseball leagues, it is typical that official scorers are not designated for regular season games. In the Major Leagues that task usually falls to a regular sportswriter for a host team's hometown newspaper. The home team usually appoints an official scorekeeper and it need not be the same person for all games of the season. However, as much as during the post-season contests, the scorer's word is law in the record books just as the umpire's calls are indisputable when in accordance with the official rulebook. The one thing I have never understood, though, is the scorer may change a hit or error call up to twelve hours following the conclusion of the game but an umpire cannot go back, for example, and say, "Oh, by the way, that pitch two pitches before that I called a ball is now actually a strike" without being chased out of Dodge on the next stagecoach.

The home team has their spectators who cheer for them and help them during the game. So does the visiting team. But the lowly umpires are basically out there all by themselves. So it's refreshing to know that, as much as possible, the official scorekeeper can be considered to be on the umpire's side . . . sometimes.

In most youth baseball leagues, the home team scorekeeper is the official scorekeeper so you want to keep that person as close to the home plate area as you can. Granted they have to relate the team's batting order to the players when they come in every inning, but I have officiated in leagues where the scorekeepers are required to sit at a picnic table located behind the backstop directly behind the home plate. She (for it is usually one of the team moms) is the only helper the umpire has outside of his field umpire in the event of a two-(or even three-) man umpire crew. She keeps tally of the runs scored, the number of outs per inning and in some cases charts the pitchers and so would know the count on the batter. I have an indicator for the count but admittedly I'm not always sure if I had already clicked off the strike for the foul ball that just bounced off the backstop behind me or the ball for the pitch in the dirt that I had to dance away from because the catcher couldn't stop it.

So, with the scorekeeper close, I can discreetly ask what's the count. Obviously we don't have electronic scoreboards at all these youth fields so the other place to keep track of the count on the batter and the number of outs in an inning is with the umpire and the scorekeepers.

When there are two or more umpires working a game, one can usually rely on the other to correct an errant count on the batter. Still, I have been known to lose the count on a batter and have to rely entirely on the scorekeeper. The previous batter grounds out to the first following a 1-0 count. When the next batter steps in, the pitcher takes his time delivering the ball. When he finally does, it sails over everyone's head for ball one. I click off one ball on my indicator without looking at it. Two pitches later we have a 2 and 1 count on the batter. But when I look at my indicator, it's showing a 3 and 1 count. Why? Because I didn't reset it to all zeroes after the ground out. Were it not for the scorekeeper to keep me honest, I would have walked this batter on only three balls.

Also, after three or four or more runs have scored in an inning, I have been known to lose count of how many outs have been made so I turn to the scorekeeper and tell her a number of outs that I know is wrong so she will correct me. I have been known to tell scorekeepers, "I've got five outs here. Now that can't be right, can it?" Nope, and she chuckles as she corrects me and we move on. Like I've said before, during game nights, I like to have a little harmless fun.

One game with a two-man umpiring crew, I felt uncomfortable when, as home plate umpire, I lost track of the count on the batter. I stood behind the catcher and in plain sight of my field umpire who was behind the pitcher with a runner on second and held my left hand out to the side to show the indicator to my partner. That is the signal between umpires, "I've lost the count."

In response, he indicated two outs. That's nice, knowing I was right with two outs but what I need to know is the count of balls and strikes on the batter. I mimicked his two out call and then held out my indicator again. My partner shook his head side to side. He didn't know the count either. I had not called time and the pitcher was ready to throw. As opposed to calling time, I hoped the batter would hit the ball fair and the issue would be moot. The throw was low and away for another ball. But how many? Then the worst possible thing occurred. The catcher asked me for the count.

"Good question," I responded and then called for time to consult with my field umpire. While still more than ten feet away, he said, "I don't have an indicator. Never keep one on the field."

That's protocol. If the field umpire had an indicator and had a wrong count he provided to a defensive player, the confusion could be devastating to the game at hand. So, with no help from there, I turned to head for the home team bench and their scorekeeper.

One of the coaches was keeping score but not pitches. "I have no idea," he admitted. "But I think there's two outs." I informed him he was correct there. I turned and walked over to the visiting team bench.

By this time it was quite obvious what I was doing and the manager met me at about their on-deck circle. "No help here," he informed me. Since nobody else knew what the count was, it would stand to reason that whatever count I gave should be accepted as no one really knew what it was. "Two balls and two strikes," I declared.

"Where do you get that?" asked the first base coach. At first I thought he was joking around at my expense but, when I waved him off as the joke I thought it was, he objected stronger. "The pitcher has only thrown three pitches. How do you get two and two?" he shouted down the baseline.

"He's thrown four," I declared, "and the count is two and two." I put the mask back on and indicated to the batter to step in.

The coach shouted down the line, "Don't step in, Paul, until I get an answer. He's only thrown three pitches." He started walking down the line to me.

"Coach," I cautioned, "I show two and two." And my indicator indeed showed two balls and two strikes, although I wasn't convinced it was right.

By this time he was near home plate. I should have run him for arguing balls and strike calls, but frankly the thought never entered my mind. "Well, I've got one and two," he countered, showing me his indicator.

I walked over to him and lowered my voice. "You saw I was looking for the count. Why didn't you say something before?"

"You never asked *me* for the count, Blue." He was right, I hadn't. But how could I be sure his count was right? I had to trust him. If he would mislead me about it, he would be smart to say it was two balls and only one strike. I accepted his count.

"Okay," I said moving away from him and raising my voice for all to hear, "Count is one and two; one ball and two strikes. Thanks." The last was directed to the coach who I now indicated he could go back to his coaching box. Our conference was done.

The next pitch was strike three so it wouldn't have mattered how many balls he had against him; he was done anyway.

And, of course, I've never had a scorekeeper ask me to speak up in making my calls because, as I said before, I want the center fielder to have no excuse at knowing the count and the number of outs. And if the center fielder can hear me, no doubt the scorekeeper (if she is within a hundred yards of the field) will hear me too. I learned very early on part of selling the authority of the call is to make it strong so there is no doubt I am totally convinced it is correct; so why should you argue?

*   *   *

Scorekeepers are not without their errors as well. To go back to the explanation of when not to score a run, there have been numerous instances where one scorekeeper might count a run as valid where the opposing team's scorekeeper might not count that same run. In the attempt to prevent that situation, I have tried during regular season games to have the scorekeepers sit together at that picnic table during the course of the game and not to have players from either team taking the attention of the scorers from their assigned tasks. So many times, in fact, it has happened that the players will rush in from their time in the field straight to the scorekeeper to find out who is up to bat and prevent her from completing the assigned tasks to finish the previous inning. Then, in the confusion, one may have 12 runs while the other team's scorekeeper records 13. While the exact score is important to them, the only time it's necessary for me as the umpire is either when it is a close game that might need to go to extra innings or a complete blow-out where I could be looking at the Mercy Rule. Often, the scorekeepers will sit in lawn chairs near their team's bench or dugout and have little conversation between the two. That's when I need to force them to talk to one another.

Around the fourth inning I will try to check with the home team scorekeeper while her team is in the field as to the score. If there are players around her, I may ask something like "Top of the fifth, right?"

Of course I'd be wrong and she would correct me. The point of asking wrong was to make her double check her page. I would then present it to her as, "But we are tied up, right?" Here is where the scorekeeper tells me the exact score for that inning. I then attempt to repeat the questions to the other team's scorekeeper if they are not sitting together. If there is a discrepancy, I let both persons know they need to get together to see who is right and what is the actual score.

There have been times (and probably a few more that I don't know about) where neither of them were actually correct and, by getting together to compare notes, each have found errors to bring their sheets together. Sometimes they need to come back to me and ask if that second run in the bottom of the first inning counted or not. Now, here it is the middle of the fourth inning and they are asking about a run three innings ago. But, you know what? I can remember it very clearly and explain the situation to these two individuals.

I will be entirely honest here when I tell you that I try to forget the previous pitch before the next one is thrown let alone if the run counted three innings before. But, somehow once I get into the zone, I could probably replay the entire game for someone if he were to ask. The one thing, though, at this level of play is that we don't count errors and balks because, in truth, if we did every pitcher could have a no-hitter. He may have surrendered eighteen runs but still pitch a no-hitter because his fielders made errors on almost every play. Dropped balls, overthrows, even wild pitches and passed balls can be counted as errors if it allows a runner to advance from when the miscue occurred.

Now, admittedly there are six sub-sections of the rulebook dealing with scoring and scorekeepers to further explain what is and what isn't an error, but that is the explanation in a nutshell.

Before I leave this tale of error, I do need to demonstrate where the rulebook contradicts itself to a degree. But it does so for clarification (and that is even more confusing when you think about it).

An error is to be recorded for any fielder's inaccurate throw allowing a runner to advance to a base safely where an accurate throw *could* have resulted in an out. Then the rulebook goes into one of those exceptions for a catcher's throw to second base so wild as not to retire a runner stealing the base shall not be counted as an error. So a catcher's overthrow to second base to nail a stealing runner would not be an error? Well, no … but yes. If that throw to second base gets loose and the runner continues to advance safely to third base, then it becomes an error.
Let's set up an example of each I have seen (and, thank the baseball gods, haven't had to clarify for a scorekeeper).

With runners on first and second, both take off once the ball passes the plate (for lead-offs in the lower age levels are not permitted until that point) and the catcher throws to second base to get the runner there. Unfortunately his throw winds up in center field and both runners are safe. Would this have been an error? By the rules it would not because the runner he was attempting to put out did not advance any further than the base he was stealing in the first place. And, because it was a double steal, the runner who wound up on third could be said to have reached the base because of defensive indifference and therefore would not be credited with a stolen base anyway. Again, thank goodness we don't keep track of statistics like this with the younger players.

Now, let's look at the same situation with runners on first and second and they both steal together. The same catcher's throw goes into center field and each runner advances one more base (to home and third). Now the throw becomes an error because of the subsequent advance of the runner or runners. Even if only the runner that initially reached third on the defensive indifference would have scored but the runner on second stayed there, it would be an error. Are you now still willing to be scorekeeper for your son's team this summer?

For fun sometime read over that section in the rulebook and try to be able to explain it to an inexperienced manager/father with the book in front of you. That would be the easier part. As an umpire, I have to know every rule in the book forwards and backwards without being able to refer to the text. Could you imagine if the umpire pulled out the rulebook at the field to answer a question? That's why we tell the managers to show us the rule they think we've just blown. "My call is right until you can prove it's not. Then just watch me back-pedal from that one."

* * *

I have to include an experience with two "H" League teams in the Ohio Hot Stove Baseball League. Frequently we have more players sign up for a team than their roster will allow. Because of the every player plays rule, the maximum a team can field is 18 but someone years ago decided the maximum should be 12. Teams were generally divided by the elementary school the kids attended. So, if you had 20 to 24 kids from the same building enroll to play, that worked out well for two teams. But, if you had more than 25 but fewer than 33, there was going to be some players cut from the rosters. These cut players then went into a pool to fill teams from other schools that might be short a few players. After all the teams were filled up, and if there were enough players remaining in the pool, a cut team would be formed. Admittedly this team was made up of players who weren't that good and not much was expected from them. But the kids wanted to play baseball and every effort was made to encourage them during the season.

Certainly this team was not going to win too many games and many of their games would end with the 10-run Mercy Rule. One year somehow there were two cut teams playing in the "H" League bracket. Frequently during the season I would have one or the other team and would do everything I could, within reason and fair play, to encourage them to do their best. As the season wound down to a finish it was merely coincidental that these two would face each other for their final contest of the season. Neither team had won a game all year and would approach the contest with identical 0 and 16 records. At the weekly umpires' meeting to get game assignments for the following week I made an unusual request. The umpires are not supposed to know the teams in their games for the week. However, many (if not most) of the umpires obtained schedules during the year and knew very well what teams would be at what fields when. Honestly I would have to count myself among those umpires.

When the Umpire-In-Chief got to the "H" League bracket, I made my request. "I understand the two cut teams are playing each other this week," I said.

Somebody kibitzed, "That ought to be a high scoring affair. At least one of the teams will win one game."

I didn't let the comments faze me as I continued, "I want that game."

"You got it," came the quick reply from the Umpire-In-Chief.

"And one other thing," I said. "I want to know when each team practices so I can go to their practices and work with them."

"You know you're not supposed to do that," he said.

"What's it gonna hurt?" somebody suggested. "If they haven't learned anything all summer, he's not going to be able to teach them much in one night."

"Okay," the U-I-C said. He then gave me the phone numbers for each manager and left it in my hands to make the contacts. Their game was Wednesday night leaving Monday and Tuesday for their practices. I let each coach know what I wanted to do and neither had an objection. Also they had scheduled their practices on opposite nights without knowing the other's intentions. The practices went well as I attempted to work with each player from each team on how to stand still in the batter's box but step into the pitch, how to get down behind the glove to field the ball and then throw in one continuous motion to the proper base. I was all over the field each night and was very tired at the end of their practices. But, each night, before we left, I gathered all the boys and coaches together and asked them the three questions: Did you have fun? Did you learn anything? Are you coming back tomorrow?

Wednesday night I was ready for the game and I know the players were ready, too. At the ground rules meeting at home plate, I told the managers, "We can play this as a scrimmage game if you want and you can have coaches on the field. You can help the boys during the game (just don't touch the ball) and we'll just have a whole lot of fun." I also told them I would be doing some coaching as well from behind the catcher and I wasn't going to try to keep track of how many times for each team.

I can't tell you who won or what the final score was. I don't even remember if we played five innings or seven but I do know it was not a mercy rule game. At the end of the games during the season, the players usually would line up at the first and third base and then cross the field to exchange their high fives in a row around the pitcher's mound. But, without being told, for this game all the players just kind of met in the area of the mound to congratulate one another on a fun game. Then came the best moment of all.

One of the players, at the top of his lungs, asked "Did we have fun tonight?" Everybody yelled their agreement. Another player shouted, "Did we learn anything tonight?" and again a resounding "Yes." The third question was presented: "Are you coming back tomorrow?" This brought a mixed response because this was the last game of the season. No more games, no more practices, no reason to come back tomorrow. So I altered Buck's question. "Are you coming back next year to play baseball?"

Everybody (and I swear even a coach or two) shouted, "Yes!"

We had a great night!

Epilogue

After Momma passed away in March 2000, Buck stayed around the house. My siblings were able to get him involved in a widow/widowers' support group and he met a wonderful woman there. Soon after they married.

They moved to Florida in 2002 to retire. Buck's health began failing, we thought because of his age. Around 2010, he was diagnosed with lung cancer. At his age of eighty-three, surgery was not recommended so he resigned himself to the expected result.

I moved to Florida in 2005, about two hour's drive south of Brooksville. I continued umpiring and wanted one more game for him to watch. He was unable to travel to see me, so I contacted the Hernando County Little League chapter and asked for the opportunity to guest officiate one of their games for Buck to see me.

This chapter uses volunteer umpires, but not just anyone could be there. I needed a referral from an Umpire-In-Chief from Manatee County. I'd established myself as a respected representative and it was arranged for April 2012.

The Saturday noon game was scheduled and arrangements made for Buck to be there. Arriving well before the start time, the host facility was ready for the special day for father and son. Buck had a place for his lawn chair right behind the backstop on the third base side. I would be in the all-too-familiar position of home plate umpire – behind the mask.

A field umpire was scheduled. But I wanted one more thing. I walked out to where Buck sat, carrying an extra umpire's shirt. "The field umpire couldn't make it today," I told him, extending the shirt. "Can you take the bases?"

At first fear enveloped his face but then, in his usual humorous self, asked, "Can I take my chair with me?" Those around us saw the levity and laughed. I gave him a hug.

During the game, I could hear people talking with Buck

but I kept my attention on the field. From my professional demeanor, I heard one spectator ask him how many years I had been umpiring. "Around forty," I heard him reply. His pride at being given such a special opportunity, to be around the ball field once again, showed in his voice and demeanor.

Between innings, I stepped back to him and asked his assessment. "You're still calling some of the pitches too quick," he observed.

"Well, I wanted to make sure I called them before you did."

Another trait I have is to get my butt down low, right on the ground if possible. This way eye-level is at the top of the young players' strike zones. The umpire positions himself in the crease between the catcher and the batter so he can see the strike zone over the plate toward the catcher. If the catcher needs to move his glove toward the batter, the pitch was out of the strike zone.

I heard one spectator ask Buck why I get down so low in my stance. "Getting down's not the hard part," he said. "It's the getting back up."

Keeping my eyes on the field, I pointed toward him with my left hand and said, "You've got that right."

One interesting play during the game involved one out with a runner on first. The batter squared to bunt but placed his right foot on the edge of home plate, completely out of the batter's box – an instant put-out. But I wasn't sure if this league enforced the rule for this youngest division. The batter/runner made it safely to first base, so I had to find out their rules.

I turned to see the Umpire-In-Chief standing behind the backstop, watching my game. I called 'Time' and stepped back to ask him about enforcement.

"Yeah, I saw that. Wondered if you picked up on it," he said.

"So you enforce it here, even at this age?"

I could see Buck get up from his chair to step over closer. He hadn't missed it either.

"Go ahead," the U-I-C said with a wave of his hand.

"Just be sure to put the other runner back on first," Buck chimed in. I knew that but I also knew some umpires might miss it. It gave Buck the opportunity to be helpful on the field. It was my turn to beam at his continued knowledge of the rules.

Afterward, I had to wonder. Was it deliberate, a staged test for me? I never asked but it was a good 'little known rule' situation. And I passed.

It was a great day for Buck and me. We got to share one more game and, as umpires do, even at this level, we rehashed the game on the way back to his house.

Dad passed away on February 1, 2013. I miss him so much.

Thank you.

Hopefully this has been as enjoyable for you to read as it was for me to walk down memory lane over the years. I've recently retired from the Grand Old Game but still get around the fields for spring ball each year here in Florida starting in February. And I will doubtless encounter more unusual and humorous situations as the young boys and girls still learn this game and have fun doing it. Just don't tell them they are learning lessons for adult life. That will be our little secret. Right, Buck?

Made in the USA
Middletown, DE
12 December 2021

55451568R00116